How To Grow An Effective Sunday School

Elmer L. Towns

ACCENT BOOKS
Denver, Colorado

ACCENT BOOKS
A division of Accent-B/P Publications, Inc.
12100 W. Sixth Avenue
P.O. Box 15337
Denver, Colorado 80215

Contents

To Jimmy Breland (with the Lord).
Of all the Sunday School teachers I had,
Jimmy Breland had the greatest influence on my life.
With eternal appreciation,

Elmer L. Towns

1 The Challenge of Sunday School

Sunday School accomplishes one of the greatest needs in the twentieth century church: education. Therefore, its ministry is imperative. Since Sunday School is biblical education in action, it is the mortar that holds the bricks together and becomes the foundation of the house.

Although most churches have larger attendance at their morning services than at their Sunday Schools, this fact does not diminish the influence of Sunday School. A few years ago one large denomination reported that almost 90 percent of their new members came from the Sunday School.

WHY THE SUNDAY SCHOOL IS VITAL

1. Sunday School is imperative because it carries out the Great Commission. The Great Commission is found in the risen Lord's parting words and recorded in Matthew 28:19-20: "Go ye therefore, and teach all nations, baptizing them in the name of the Father, and of the Son, and of the Holy Ghost: Teaching them to observe all things whatsoever I have commanded you: and, lo, I am with you alway, even unto the end of the world." Jesus told us to reach, teach, and win the lost.

Sunday School carries out all three of these

commands but the ultimate step of the Great Commission is "... teaching them to observe...." Reaching is the foundation of evangelism, but teaching involves knowing, understanding, and responding. A person is not converted until he recognizes, understands, and responds to the gospel. A new Christian must know what to believe and how to behave. Before a person can be baptized, he has to receive the Word and be converted. Then, "they that gladly received his word were baptized..." (Acts 2:41). Therefore, teaching becomes a mandatory step in presenting the gospel. When we neglect the important function of follow-up teaching, we have not carried out the Great Commission.

There are trends in the twentieth century church that will weaken Christianity and spell the ruin of churches. Some churches are building on emotions and music; there is little Bible teaching. Other churches are building on the dynamic personality of their pastor; they, too, have little Bible teaching. There are still other trends among churches: some base their ministry on music, missionary outreach; or their action-oriented ministry to youth is the catalyst of the church. Finally, some traditional churches continue their ministry on the habit that people have of attending Sunday morning services.

All of these trends have a legitimate place in the church's ministry. But they have neglected the heart of the Great Commission. Jesus said, "Go ye therefore, and teach . . . teaching them to observe all things. . . ." Teaching is the imperative need of our twentieth century churches. The church that builds on the Sunday School is strengthened because the Sunday School is where teaching the Bible is predominant.

2. *Sunday School is imperative because it teaches God's Word systematically*. The Sunday School is the only place in most churches that gives a systematic, comprehensive, complete coverage of the Word of God.

As good as Bible preaching in the morning service is, sermons are usually selective and do not systematically cover the Bible. Sermons also are usually motivational, aimed at changing the life rather than systematically communicating Bible doctrine and content.

Training classes do not emphasize Bible content to a great extent, although they use the Bible. The same can be said of children's club programs such as Awana, Pioneer Girls, and Christian Service Brigade. Children's Church programs are usually more motivational than instructional.

Sunday School lessons, however, follow a pre-determined curriculum. These lessons are planned by specialists in Christian education who are concerned that equal treatment be given to every subject according to the importance it has in Scripture and the influence it can make on a life. Some curriculums plan to cover the Bible every four years, others in seven years, and some once in the lifetime of a student. Regular Sunday School attendance is important for every believer so that he might gain a full knowledge of Bible content and doctrine.

3. *Sunday School is imperative for growth toward maturity.* The aim of a Christian is maturity—"For the perfecting of the saints, for the work of the ministry, for the edifying of the body of Christ: Till we all come in the unity of the faith, and of the knowledge of the Son of God, unto a perfect man, unto the measure of the stature of the fulness of Christ: That we henceforth be no more children, tossed to and fro, and carried about with every wind of doctrine, by the sleight of men, and cunning craftiness, whereby they lie in wait to deceive; But speaking the truth in love, may grow up into him in all things, which is the head, even Christ" (Ephesians 4:12-15).

When a Christian reaches full maturity, he is

complete or whole. Every part of his life is integrated around Christ. In personality, this involves knowledge, skills, attitude, and habits. In Bible knowledge, this involves a foundational knowledge of every doctrine and a basic introduction to Scripture. In service, this involves using his gifts according to the ability God gave him.

The Bible has the tremendous power to: change individuals and nations, "for the word of God is quick, and powerful . . ." (Hebrews 4:12); convict of sin (Jeremiah 23:29); draw a sinner to Christ (John 6:63, 68); convert the soul (Psalm 19:7); implant faith (Romans 10:17); produce a new nature (II Peter 1:4); strengthen babes (I Peter 2:2); fortify growth (Hebrews 5:12, 13); and equip Christians for battle (Ephesians 6:12).

But knowledge about Christianity has little value unless the Holy Spirit applies it to the heart. The pupil must understand and obey the precepts of the Bible. People become hardened Pharisees when the Bible is a mere academic textbook. Therefore, the Bible must be taught by spiritual teachers, using biblical methods, empowered by the Holy Spirit, and guided by the Great Commission.

The main function of Sunday School is to teach the Bible according to God's methods. Through its classes, the dynamic gospel can make an impact on individuals, nurturing them toward maturity, and hence on communities, bringing revival to a nation.

4. Sunday School is imperative to protect the church's future. Those who are born again will drift in their commitment to Christ if they do not have objective teaching to anchor their faith. Their sinful nature, the temptations of Satan, and the snare of the world will erode Bible doctrine or purity of life. A Bible-teaching Sunday School is necessary to preserve a biblical church.

Also, children born into Christian homes must be prepared to carry on when their parents pass off the scene. They must be brought to a saving knowledge of Christ and be equipped to be leaders when they come of age. Since a church will naturally die with time, Sunday School education is imperative to carry on the future of the church.

WHAT IS SUNDAY SCHOOL?

Most people mistakenly think that Sunday School is a few classes for children in the basement of the church before the important meeting—the Sunday morning service. How wrong this is! Every member of the family should be in Sunday School because every person should be growing spiritually and learning the Word of God.

Sunday School is not just an appendage tacked on before or after the morning church service. Sunday School is an arm of the church. Just as the arm is part of the body and a person is not complete without an arm, so no church is complete without a Sunday School.

The Sunday School should be constituted by the church and should operate under its control. It should carry out the aims of the church and receive its ministry from the congregation.

The verse that has historically been used to describe the ministry of the Sunday School is Deuteronomy 31:12: "Gather the people together, men, and women, and children, and thy stranger that is within thy gates, that they may hear, and that they may learn, and fear the Lord your God, and observe to do all the words of this law."

Notice the three aspects of Sunday School in this verse:

1. Sunday School is the reaching arm of the church.

The command first directs that people be gathered. This is the ministry of reaching people for Jesus Christ: men, women, children, and strangers (those outside the church). Note the command did not begin with children; so Sunday Schools that have mostly children in attendance have not properly applied the Scriptures. Sunday School is a family institution first, next reaching out to the unsaved (the stranger).

In both the Old and the New Testaments, God commands His people to reach out of the assembly to the unsaved—"Gather the people. . . ." Sunday School has traditionally been a gathering arm of people, both saved and unsaved, who were brought for Christian instruction. The verse implies a central point of assembly. (The word *church* comes from *assembly*.) Therefore, Sunday School is fulfilling a biblical mandate when people are brought together for instruction.

The word *reaching* is defined as making contact with persons and motivating them to give an honest hearing to the gospel. Sunday Schools can reach all types of people at all ages through organized visitation, attendance campaigns, advertisements, newsletters, or simply every person sharing Jesus Christ with his friends. Reaching is evangelism in action.

2. Sunday School is the teaching arm of the church. For people to be born again, the Word of God must be planted in their hearts. "Being born again, not of corruptible seed, but of incorruptible, by the word of God, which liveth and abideth for ever" (I Peter 1:23). The Bible is likened to seed (Mark 4:14), and when it is planted in the heart, God begins the work of regeneration. The Word of God enlightens the blind (Psalm 19:8), and leads a person to Jesus Christ (I Thessalonians 2:13).

Therefore, when Sunday Schools inculcate the Word of God in the heart, they are preparing people for salvation. But Sunday School is more than just an evangelistic tool; the Word of God is taught to all Christians. They grow because the Bible nourishes them.

Teachers must faithfully communicate the Bible lessons. When they teach children, the Bible must be presented at the children's level. When they teach adults the Word of God, they must challenge the mentality of adults. This principle of communication has been called *reaching men where they are and, through teaching, lifting them to where they should be.*

The role of teaching is explained in Deuteronomy 31:12: "...That they may hear, and ... learn ...." The first step of teaching, then, is hearing. A person must be presented with the gospel; he must hear the gospel. Even then he may reject, but he cannot make a decision on the gospel until he has heard it. The ultimate step in teaching is *learning.* There is no teaching until the pupils have learned the lessons. When a Sunday School is called the teaching arm of the church, it has not fulfilled its function until people have learned the Word of God.

3. *Sunday School is the winning arm of the church.* The purpose of reaching and teaching is to win people to Jesus Christ. Our verse describing the ministry of Sunday School continues to say, "... That they may ... fear the Lord your God ..." The phrase, "fear the Lord," is an Old Testament term of salvation. Other phrases—trust, believe, receiving Jesus Christ—have the same meaning.

THE RESULTS OF SUNDAY SCHOOL

The value of Sunday School is immeasurable. The church that has a growing, vital Sunday School has a New Testament foundation on which it can build. Many other ministries are needed to complete the church—youth programs, revival meetings, music programs, training meetings, children's clubs—but without a Sunday School a church will have a difficult time building for the future. Some advantages of the Sunday School are as follows:

1. Evangelistic influence on the neighborhood. One important objective of the Sunday School is to saturate its neighborhood with the gospel (Acts 5:28, 42). This involves organized visitation, every Sunday School class visiting those who should be in its class. Most Sunday Schools set aside a week night for organized visitation. This involves a training class where workers are taught how to visit; then the trained workers are assigned responsibility for the evening. With real persistence workers go out to reach their neighbors for Christ.

It is also mandatory that every absentee be contacted. Every lesson has aims and material that is vital, just as spokes in a wheel are necessary to give the wheel strength and keep it from collapsing. Every pupil should hear every lesson to have a complete Christian life. When a pupil is absent, he is missing something from the well-rounded Bible curriculum that has been prepared. Teachers should therefore visit him when he is absent to insure his attendance the following week.

But visitation is not just a cheerful call in the home to encourage continuing attendance. The teacher should teach or at least summarize the missed lesson and answer any questions that may arise. This helps to nip backsliding in the bud in the lives of those with little spiritual concern.

2. Harvesting opportunity of the lost. A Sunday School that is reaching its community will have visitors attending its classes. Some of these will have no church affiliation and usually little training in the Word of God.

They represent a rich potential for harvest. If a Sunday School has a well-planned, carefully executed program of evangelism, it will win many to Jesus Christ.

3. Doctrinal stability in the church. Through the curriculum the Bible should be taught in Sunday School as the complete, authoritative, infallible revelation from God to man. It is the basis for the student's personal relationship to Jesus Christ and the means for his daily growth in grace. The student must see that the Word of God supplies consistent doctrine for faith and guidance in every experience of life.

Doctrine ultimately increases our love for Christ, causing us to grow into His image. Good doctrine protects a church from heresy and from the cooling of its first love (Revelation 2:4).

4. In-service training for Christians. The Sunday School must be organized for its reaching, teaching, winning program. Therefore, a well-planned and carefully executed program is necessary for its success. This necessitates training an entire staff of workers.

First, the structure must be planned; next, workers must be recruited and then trained concerning their qualifications and duties. This involves supervisors, secretaries, teachers, and those involved in evangelistic outreach. Trained workers will guarantee a quality Sunday School. These workers contribute to the total maturity of the local church.

5. Total church growth. Since the work of Sunday School and morning service is harmonious, both contributing to a New Testament church, they are interrelated and indivisible. A strong Sunday School builds a strong local church. The same people attend the morning service who attend the Sunday School; therefore, those who are taught in Sunday School make better worshipers in the morning service. In this way, the total church is strengthened.

6. Christian responsibility in the community. The Sunday School trains and motivates pupils to witness in the community. But more than evangelism, Sunday School pupils make a cooperative expression of moral righteousness in the community. Their godly influence is felt in their local areas: home, school, business, city activities, and life in general. Since Christians are the salt of the earth (Matthew 5:13), a Sunday School should make people thirsty for the gospel.

7. Missionary influence around the world. Since Sunday Schools seek to lead their pupils into a dedicated life to obey all of God's commands, pupils cannot deny the Great Commission. Ultimately, the obligation of home and foreign missions will be felt in the Sunday School. Pupils will respond by praying, giving, and going into all the world. Missions involves more than crossing an ocean; it involves home missions, which can mean work in Sunday School missions, rescue missions, summer missionary endeavors, and other ministries beyond the local community.

SUMMARY

The Sunday School is imperative as the reaching, teaching, winning arms of the church. When it fulfills these purposes through Christian education, it enlarges the church, influences the community, and reaches the world.

GUIDE QUESTIONS FOR STUDY AND DISCUSSION

1. Sunday School is important because it carries out what great need in today's church?

2. How does Sunday School carry out the Great Commission?
3. Why is the command to teach of special significance in the Great Commission?
4. Name some ways the Sunday School aids in the Christian's growth toward maturity.
5. If a church neglects its Sunday School how can the church's future be affected?
6. Explain how Deuteronomy 31:12 describes the three aspects of the Sunday School's ministry.
7. In what ways will a growing, Bible-teaching Sunday School affect the church, its community, and the world?

ACTIVITIES FOR FURTHER STUDY AND APPLICATION

1. Consider how you can strengthen the Sunday School's worth in the view of your congregation.
2. Examine your present Sunday School curriculum, keeping in mind the three basic commands of Deuteronomy 31:12. Prepare a list of areas in which you feel it needs strengthening to consider as you proceed in this study.

RESOURCES

Barnette, J. N., *The Pull of the People* (Convention Press, Nashville, 1956).

Leavitt, Guy D., *Teaching With Success* (Standard Publishing Company, Cincinnati, OH, 1956).

Towns, Elmer L., *The Successful Sunday School and Teachers Guidebook* (Creation House, Carol Stream, IL 1976).

Towns, Elmer L., *The Ten Largest Sunday Schools and What Makes Them Grow* (Baker Book House, Grand Rapids, MI, 1969).

2 Organizing the Sunday School

The title *Sunday School* is not found in the Bible; however, its function is there for it carries out the aim and program that God intends for the church to teach all of the Bible to all people. To do this Sunday School needs to be organized for efficient working. God controls His universe by order and design; the Sunday School should do no less.

God's organization is evident in the arrangement of the Creation and its continuing function. The tribes of Israel were organized around the tabernacle in the wilderness. Jesus also operated out of strategy. When our Lord preached so long the great crowd became hungry, His disciples served food in an organized plan as He directed. When the 70 were sent out to minister, they went out two by two, according to a program. The early church went through Jerusalem systematically: "And daily in the temple, and in every house, they ceased not to teach and preach Jesus Christ" (Acts 5:42). Paul taught priority and order in the church in I Corinthians 12:28, then commanded the church: "Let all things be done decently and in order" (I Corinthians 14:40).

While the Sunday School gets its authority from the Word of God, it functions through the local church. Every church organization has some type of church government which is stated in the church constitution, and the Sunday School is no exception. Every Sunday School officer, teacher, and worker should be made aware of the church constitution as it refers to the Sunday School and how his work relates to the total church ministry.

THE WHOLE BIBLE FOR ALL PEOPLE

1. Teaching according to age and needs. Our grandparents attended a country school where all eight grades were assembled in one room. There were advantages and disadvantages to this large, homogeneous crowd from age six to fourteen. Later, our fathers attended a consolidated school with each age meeting in separate rooms so education could be geared to individual needs. Today, there are more advanced schools with classes specializing in subject matter and teaching methods which are adapted to the individual, special needs of pupils.

Today's Sunday Schools should also be organized to carefully minister to all the needs of those in the church family. The pupils in the Sunday School should be divided into classes as closely representing their ages as possible, without the classes becoming too small or too large.

Historically, the first Sunday School class was the *primary class,* taken from the word *primer,* the name of an early textbook. Later, a younger class was added where children "began"; hence, the class was called the *beginners.* If a child were halfway between childhood and adulthood he was called a *junior.* Later, the name *intermediate* was used for those halfway between junior and adult. Today, for the most part, Sunday Schools use the terminology children are used to in their school life: Nursery, Kindergarten, Primary, Junior, Junior High,

High School. College and Career people, as well as Young Marrieds are grouped as Young Adults. Then there are Adult classes and Senior Citizen classes. Some churches will have all of these groups; others will have a limited number or some adaptation of them.

2. *Teaching according to content.* Also back in granddad's school, everyone "heard" the same lesson because there was only one teacher to listen to pupils recite their lessons. Regardless of their need, most pupils endured the lessons of other pupils. It was easy to lose interest when lessons were too advanced or too simple.

In early Sunday Schools, everyone listened to the lesson taught to the whole assembled Sunday School. Even after the Sunday School met in separate departments, the whole school studied the same "uniform" lesson, regardless of age. Today, there should be a Sunday School class for every age, with content written to the needs, background, and the degree of understanding of the pupil.

In essence, every teacher must become a specialist in teaching the Word of God to one particular age. That teacher is the shepherd of that class. Hence, the teacher can use the best teaching methods for the age level, and the pupils can comprehend the whole Bible in a systematic and interesting manner.

PLANNING FOR GROWTH

Most Sunday Schools fall within one of the three sizes and kinds of organizations: the Class-Graded Sunday School, the Departmentally-Graded Sunday School, and the Age-Graded Sunday School. As a Sunday School grows through each of these phases, it faces certain strengths and weaknesses.

1. *The Class-Graded Sunday School.* This Sunday

School is organized around individual classes. For Sunday Schools with an approximate attendance of 100, there are usually ten classes (see the Sunday School Organization Chart). Bed babies and toddlers should be in Nursery Care. The Preschool Class includes toddlers as they become two years old and the three year olds. Four and five year olds are no longer the "beginners" in Sunday School. They have their important place in Sunday School as Kindergartners.

The Primary Class is comprised of children six, seven, and eight years old in first, second and third grades in school. For the Junior Class, children nine, ten, and eleven in grades four, five, and six, Sunday School leaders have historically divided the boys and girls into different rooms or classes. This is no longer a standard procedure because children are placed together in public schools.

The Junior High School Class should reflect the division in the local public schools. If grades seven through nine are organized in a central junior high school building, your Sunday School should reflect the same. If, however, your local junior high school involves only seventh and eighth grades, the young people will want to be grouped socially with their peers. There is a problem to face with curriculum materials, which will be discussed in the chapter on curriculum.

There is diversity in organizing adults. It may be difficult to attract enough college and career people in the small church to form a separate class for them, but it is wise to try to preserve the new high school graduates in Sunday School by having such a class ready for them. They may need to be combined with young marrieds as a Young Adult Class. Next, an Adult Bible Class is a necessity. Churches differ regarding whether men and women are in combined or separate classes. Most Sunday Schools divide senior citizens into the men's and

GROW AN EFFECTIVE SUNDAY SCHOOL

Sunday School Organization Chart

AGE	0 1	2 3	4 5	6 7 8	9 10 11
GRADE				1 2 3	4 5 6
CLASS-GRADED Sunday School Attendance: 100	(Nursery Care 0-1)	Preschool Class	Kindergarten Class	Primary Class	Junior Class (Boys & Girls together)
Percent of Attendance	7%	7%	8%	15%	18%
DEPARTMEN-TALLY-GRADED Sunday School Attendance: 250-350	Cribs & Toddlers	2 Preschool Classes	Open Session One Room 4 tables - - - - - Traditional 1 Dept. 4 classes	Open Session One Room 6 tables - - - - - Traditional 1 Dept. 6 classes	Open Session One Room 6 tables - - - - - Traditional 1 Dept. 6 Classes
AGE-GRADED Sunday School Attendance: 400-1,000	4 Nurseries	4 Preschool Classes	Open Session Rooms One Class for each Age Level 6 tables per classroom	Open Session Rooms One Class for each Age Level 8-9 tables per classroom	

12 13 14	15 16 17	18 24	25 60	Senior Citizen	
7 8 9	10 11 12	College			
Junior High Class	High School Class	Young Adults	Adult Class	Women's Class	Men's Class
12%		40%			
Junior High Dept. 7th Grade Class 8th Grade Class 9th Grade Class	High School Dept. 10th Grade Class 11th Grade Class 12th Grade Class	College-Career Young Married Special Classes	Adult Dept. Organized Electives Age-Graded	Women's Classes	Men's Classes
One Class per Age Level 5-7 workers for each class		Classes organized for each age level of adults			

women's classes.

The Sunday School with a class for each division, however, is intended only as a beginning point and should be considered as a temporary measure. Every effort should be made to expand each class by reaching the lost for Jesus Christ. As classes grow, divide them so that individual needs can be better met and age groups can be better taught.

2. *Departmentally-Graded Sunday School.* This Sunday School is organized around departments. Today there are two approaches to grading by departments. The *traditional approach* gathers all the pupils in the department for an opening assembly; then the pupils are divided into four or six smaller classes, each having one teacher with approximately 8-10 pupils per class. Small rooms are provided for uninterrupted teaching sessions.

The advantages are the emphasis on personalized instruction and more thorough methods of follow-up. The difficulties of departmental grading are the expense of providing a room each time approximately ten new pupils are recruited for the Sunday School and recruitment of an adequate number of teachers.

The second use of departmental grading is *open-session* teaching. A large room (usually 24' x 36') houses a department/class. The department/class uses all the space for the entire educational hour. The superintendent acts in the role of head teacher leading the session, with several assistant teachers stationed around teaching tables in the room. There are no divisions between the tables; all of the teachers work in harmony leading the learning activities.

A department/class usually averages approximately 25-60 in attendance. A Sunday School usually has from five to eight departments, with the total Sunday School average attendance being between 200-350.

As the Sunday School grows, it is wise to slowly

move organizationally from a class-graded to a depart-mental Sunday School. Usually a department is added first among preschool and kindergarten students; next, departments are added at the elementary level; and, finally, they are added in the youth division.

No rigid formula can be set because the age spread in Sunday Schools is different. The number of children in Sunday School is usually based on two factors: (1) the number of buses in operation, and (2) the age of the married adults attending.

3. Age-Graded Sunday School. The departmental Sunday School will reach the upper limits of 400 pupils, and the departments must be subdivided if growth is to continue. There should be a department (either traditional or open-session) for each school grade. There will be approximately 25 in each age-graded department.

There is little difficulty in dividing ages while children are in school; the problem comes with adults. Some Sunday Schools divide adults into five-year departments. However, there are problems with dividing adults by their age. For example, are they promoted when the age of the husband advances or that of the wife? Too, some adults prefer not to be identified by age.

To counter these problems, some Sunday Schools have extensive elective programs for adults; others have organized classes around teacher personalities, and still others loosely grade adult ages. There are several plans and each Sunday School must make its own decision concerning which it will follow.

Watch for the danger levels of growth. Most Sunday Schools reach a natural plateau when they reach the upper levels of their present type of organization. It is difficult, for instance, to push Sunday School growth past 150 with a class-graded plan and many Sunday Schools stay around that figure because they have not provided for growth. There must be more organizational supervision, more space (perhaps new buildings), and more classes formed, as well as enough teachers to insure individual ministry when each plateau of growth has been reached.

One of the most difficult growth hurdles for a Sunday School is bridging the gap from a class-graded Sunday School to a departmentally-graded Sunday School. Techniques that will overcome this danger level are: (1) expanding class size into open-session teaching; (2) providing new, larger rooms; and (3) establishing an adequate teacher training program that will provide more Sunday School workers for expansion.

BALANCING EXPERIENCE AND CONTENT

Jesus reminded us that "they that worship him must worship him in spirit and in truth" (John 4:24b). The word *truth* is Bible content. There must be adequate time spent in Sunday School on recognizing, learning, and memorizing Bible facts. But, if left to itself, this would lead to dead orthodoxy. There must be the working of the Spirit in the experience of teacher and pupil alike. Pupils must feel, touch, and express the biblical truth. This involves group discussion, handcrafts, and other activities for total involvement in the learning process.

Experience at one time was tacked on to the first of the Bible lesson and called "opening exercise." This period involved singing, special music, testimonies, and some type of visual lesson. A better way is to incorporate these activities into the total lesson.

SUMMARY

The Sunday School is the arm of the church to carry

out the Great Commission by reaching, teaching, and winning all ages to Christ. The Sunday School, at times, has been separate from the church, but this fragments its results and dilutes its aim. The Sunday School must work in harmony with the local church, just as a person's arm must correlate its function with the rest of the body.

To carry out the New Testament aim, the Sunday School must divide people into classes according to their educational background, their needs, and their ability to understand the lesson. This is done by class-graded Sunday Schools, departmental Sunday Schools, and age-graded Sunday Schools.

GUIDE QUESTIONS FOR STUDY AND DISCUSSION

1. What was the first Sunday School class and how did it get its name?
2. List and describe the three types of Sunday School organization.
3. What are the two approaches to grading by department?
4. What is the suggested method for moving from a class-graded to a departmentally-graded Sunday School?
5. What are the three techniques to overcome danger levels in Sunday School growth?

ACTIVITIES FOR FURTHER STUDY AND APPLICATION

1. Classify your type of Sunday School organization and note how close you are to a danger level in growth.
2. Map out a specific plan of action for moving past that danger level into the next phase of Sunday School

development.

RESOURCES

Benson, Clarence H., *Sunday School Success* (Evangelical Teacher Training Association, Wheaton, IL, 1964, revised).

Towns, Elmer L., *The Successful Sunday School and Teachers Guidebook* (Creation House, Carol Stream, IL, 1976).

3 Administrating
the Sunday School

Many Sunday Schools have a great desire to reach the lost in their community and teach them the Word of God but fail to do so. As Sunday Schools have faced new frontiers, they have stumbled over their machinery and were not able to go forward. The Sunday School must be properly organized for a spiritual thrust just as a business, army or any other institution organizes itself for new thrusts. The success of the organization, however, depends to a large extent upon the way it is administered.

THE PLACE OF THE PASTOR

"Like priest, like people" applies both to the pulpit and to the teaching ministry of the pastor. While in some churches the pastor is the administrator of the Sunday School, in the majority of cases there is a separate officer in the form of a general superintendent. In either case, and whether he intentionally strives to do so or not, the pastor sets the tone for the church's attitude toward its Sunday School. He is not only its spiritual head because of his pulpit ministry to its members, but he is also its example in life and in his recognition of the importance of Sunday School.

In magnifying the Sunday School, the pastor is

silently saying to all of its workers and students, "I appreciate you. You are vital to the life of the church. It is my desire to do everything in my power to aid in your ministry."

As local churches grow, their supervisory needs tend to mushroom and more leaders must assume responsibility. The pastor cannot and should not spend all his time looking after the small details of running the Sunday School. He needs administrative assistants, such as a superintendent and perhaps an assistant superintendent, to make sure that the total Sunday School is properly functioning. Some churches have been so conditioned that they want the pastor to do it all. However, leadership is getting the job done through other people.

In times past, a Sunday School committee/cabinet was organized to administer the ministry of the Sunday School. This committee was made up of the pastor, the Sunday School superintendent, and other elected personnel. With the growth of the total educational program in modern churches, however, a broader committee was needed to give leadership to the total ministry of education in the local church. Today the Board of Christian Education has grown to assume this ministry, including the supervision of Sunday School. The pastor is a member of the Board of Christian Education, along with other godly people from the educational groups in the church. The pastor always remains vitally involved in the Sunday School because working through the Sunday School is one of the best ways he can shepherd the total church.

THE BOARD OF CHRISTIAN EDUCATION

The manifold purpose of the Board of Christian

Education is to carry out the teaching obligation in the Great Commission through the local church; to provide representative influence from the church into the Sunday School; to prevent omissions in the program, overlapping of content, and over-emphasis on any one topic; to effectively correlate and coordinate the total Christian education program; to approve educational curriculum and materials; to suggest the educational budget; to determine qualifications and personnel for teaching positions; and to evaluate the present program with a view of planning for the future educational needs of the church.

In keeping with its purpose, the Board counsels, maps out programs, approves curriculum materials, assesses needs, and makes plans for carrying out the educational program of the church. The organizational chart, "The Sunday School and the Board of Christian Education," shows the relationship of the Sunday School to the Board of Christian Education and its cooperative position among other educational groups in the church. It is obvious, therefore, that the Sunday School should never be a separate agency from the church; rather it is a working arm of the church.

THE SUNDAY SCHOOL STAFF

To properly administer the work of the Sunday School, the staff will consist of some or all the following members, according to the size of the school and its needs in its present state of growth: A general superintendent (an assistant superintendent if needed), department superintendents (and assistants if needed), teachers, secretary/treasurer (and department secretaries and treasurers if needed), other workers such as memory secretaries, etc.

The Sunday School and the Board of Christian Education

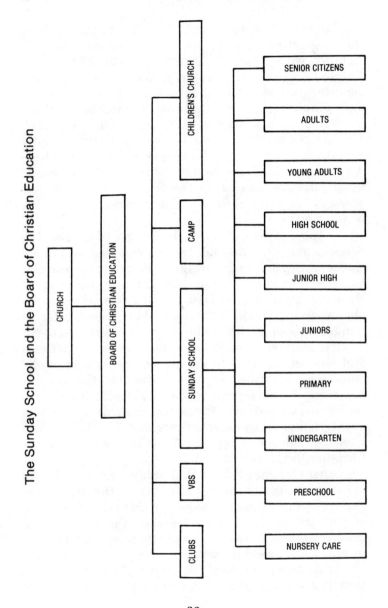

The best word to describe how the Sunday School staff should relate is *together*. "For we are labourers together with God" (I Corinthians 3:9). The pastor, Christian education director, general superintendent, departmental superintendents, and all other workers and teachers in the Sunday School must work harmoniously to build a New Testament Sunday School. The scriptural concept for leadership could be aptly visualized by a chain with each worker forming one link. A chain is no stronger than its weakest link. The whole administrative success in the Sunday School breaks down at the point of failure of one worker to fulfill his responsibility.

1. Appointment of staff. The quality of the Sunday School's ministry depends, to a great degree, on the choice of the individual workers. Before that, securing qualified workers depends on the very method of choosing them. The church which takes seriously its obligation to provide the best possible leadership for its Sunday School is already on the road toward success.

The method of selection of Sunday School officers and teachers is usually defined in the bylaws of the church constitution. In some churches the general superintendent is elected by the congregation (or church board or Christian Education Board) and he is authorized to select other officers and the teachers and workers, subject to approval by the pastor and/or Christian Education Board.

Other churches believe that because Sunday School is not an entity in itself but is an arm of the church, the church as a whole has some responsibility for the choice of its leaders. They therefore elect the officers and teachers, either annually or when there is a vacancy in a position or a teaching post.

Advocates in favor of the annual election maintain that it gives opportunity for more people to serve; it eliminates undesirable teachers and officers with less confusion; and it brings fresher ideas into the classrooms. On the other side, those who would place teachers in lifetime positions point out that teachers who are specialists become increasingly efficient as they continue to study and add to their library and resources on the same age level.

If the election is annual, the church may have an annually-appointed nominating committee. It is their responsibility to interview and enlist prospective teachers. The pastor, Sunday School superintendent, and/or the Christian education director should carefully interview each candidate. They should obtain the agreement of the candidate to the Standard or whatever form of teaching requirements they subscribe to (See Chapter 7, "Establishing Sunday School Standards.") Laxness and failure at this point may spell teacher drop-outs or pupil disinterest later.

2. Responsibilities of the general superintendent. Because the important ministry of Sunday School is reaching, teaching, and winning people to Jesus Christ, the choice of the superintendent of the Sunday School is as important as the aims. Actually, the pastor leads the church in its total ministry, but when it comes to giving direction to the Sunday School the superintendent is the supervisory link in the chain of command. Therefore, he must be a spiritual leader that personifies the spirit of the Sunday School.

(a) The Sunday School superintendent is, first of all, an administrator. He must see that the qualified teacher is scheduled in the proper classroom at the appropriate time with the correct equipment and aids to teach the assigned curriculum.

(b) The Sunday School superintendent is responsible for personnel. He must recruit new workers, make recommendations for placement, provide training, and evaluate the effectiveness of those already in service.

(c) The Sunday School superintendent supervises the ordering of literature and teaching aids, in addition to making all expenditures for the Sunday School.

(d) The Sunday School superintendent is responsible for outreach and growth. This involves visitation, follow-up of absentees, enlargement campaigns, and the application of the laws of Sunday School growth.

(e) The Sunday School superintendent is responsible for public relations. He supervises advertisement, outreach, and solves problems as they arise.

(f) The Sunday School superintendent is charged with evaluations for improvement of the entire program. He must know the standards and understand how they can be implemented.

The list of procedures that would help a superintendent carry out his responsibilities could be book length. The following suggestions will introduce some ideas to help him make the Sunday School function more efficiently.

The general superintendent should construct a yearly planning calendar that shows the times when new programs will be introduced. This should hang in the Sunday School office, along with a personnel chart which shows every position and the name of the person who fills that responsibility. Blanks on the chart tell a superintendent his personnel needs.

A superintendent needs a set of pigeonholes (mail-boxes) for ease in communication with all his staff. He should write out a job description for each position and a manual to reflect the policy by which the Sunday School operates.

The superintendent should plan a one-day conference with his staff at the beginning of each year. Here they coordinate the planning calendar, evaluate needs, inform new staff members of policy, and rally enthusiasm for the Sunday School.

3. The department superintendent. Since the department superintendent is responsible for individual classes and the interests of the total department, he or she has a relationship both to individual teachers and to the general superintendent. The larger the Sunday School, the greater his task.

A church may have both a superintendent and a director of Christian education, but neither of these have the direct supervision of the separate departments. Both administration of the department and training of his teachers are the responsibility of the department superintendent. He must be alert to departmental strengths and weaknesses and take steps to remedy the latter, bearing in mind that his department is one cog in the wheel of the entire Sunday School program.

(a) Qualifications. Occasionally the concept of a department superintendent is that of a person who makes sure that each class has a teacher and who distributes the literature, receives the offering, and takes attendance. Actually, the superintendent of a department should know the age-group characteristics and be as familiar with the best curriculum materials for them as the individual teacher of a class within the department. In addition, every specification for the general superintendent applies also to the department superintendent.

(b) Duties.

The department superintendent must promote the interest and activities of his department. He has general administrative responsibilities and is accountable for the efficient operation of his department. In meetings of the committee that guides the Sunday School, he speaks for his teachers as plans are formulated for the entire Sunday School.

The department superintendent is to plan effective assembly programs. In the traditional Sunday School, he is responsible for the opening exercises, the first 15 minutes. Here he leads the pupils in a worship program, prepares the pupils for the lesson, or reinforces the theme of the day. He gives special attention to correlation. He does not feel the necessity of being the only participant in such a worship service; he involves pupils or teachers. In the open-session approach to teaching, he assumes the role of master teacher. He guides in activities that will enhance learning. Instead of putting all activities at the beginning of the session, he places them throughout the lesson.

Tho department superintendent should conduct meetings of the department's teachers and officers. Regular meetings should allow discussion of problems within the department as a whole and the classes individually.

The department superintendent should know the standards of the total Sunday School and the program within his jurisdiction. He should evaluate accomplishments and be ready to prescribe and initiate training sessions or private conferences to remedy any undesirable situations within the department.

The department superintendent should preserve departmental morale. In his meetings with the teachers of the department, as well as in private conversations, the superintendent should convey appreciation and encouragement to them. His interest in the pupils, and his enthusiasm in approaching his programs as well as his meetings with the teachers, will all contribute toward esprit de corps.

4. *The secretary/treasurer.* It has been said that statistics have faces. The role of the secretary/treasurer is vital to the success of the Sunday School. Progress is measured by statistics, and the secretary/treasurer is

the one with the access and the ability to compile such statistics. In large churches, two people will function in these offices, one secretary and one treasurer, while one person is sufficient for both roles in small Sunday Schools.

Many times, tucked away in a four-by-four room with only one desk covered with department record books, this officer may be unknown to the majority of the membership of the Sunday School. The secretary/treasurer is often a quiet person who is unwilling to take any public part in the work of the church; nevertheless, he renders some of its most valuable service.

(a) Qualifications. He must like working with numbers and figures and be neat and accurate in computing and recording them. He must be sold on the value of the records thus carefully maintained.

(b) Duties. In the smaller church, there may be only one secretary who will compile records for the whole Sunday School. Larger schools need department secretaries who, in turn, send their reports to the general secretary. The secretary/treasurer also records minutes of any Sunday School business meetings and handles Sunday School correspondence. In letters to other churches or to community organizations the secretary actually becomes the public relations representative of the church. He should be aware of the importance of making each letter of good quality, reflecting the high standards of the church.

Each week the secretary/treasurer will prepare the statistics showing totals of enrollment, attendance, and offerings. These statistics will show leaders at a glance their strengths and weaknesses, where attendance is decreasing or where enrollment is static. Good records will sound alarms as well as herald encouragement.

SUMMARY

For an efficiently functioning Sunday School there must be good organization and supervision. The Sunday School receives its supervisory authority from the local church, which uses the Board of Christian Education to give it direction.

Beginning with the pastor and moving down, every worker must be qualified, trained, and excited about his ministry. When the leaders function properly, the whole Sunday School usually goes well.

GUIDE QUESTIONS FOR STUDY AND DISCUSSION

1. Why is the pastor's attitude the key to Sunday School success?
2. Why is organization important in the Sunday School?
3. Name several functions of the Board of Christian Education.
4. What leaders are needed to administer a growing Sunday School?
5. Who is the most important link in the concept of the Sunday School leadership as a chain?
6. Besides knowing how to be an administrator, what must the department leader know about his department?
7. Name three duties of the department superintendent.
8. Why are Sunday School records important?
9. What are two qualifications of the secretary/treasurer?

ACTIVITIES FOR FURTHER STUDY AND APPLICATION

1. Analyze your present Sunday School organization and list ways it can be improved.
2. Consult the bylaws of your church constitution and determine the method of selection of Sunday School officers and teachers in your church. In the light of this lesson, consider whether you think this method is the best for your school.
3. If you are a department superintendent, prepare a list of qualifications and duties of the teachers and officers in the department. Include a checklist of their responsibilities.
4. Prepare a list of books of in-service research and training by officers and teachers.

RESOURCES

Benson, Clarence H., *Sunday School Success* (Evangelical Teacher Training Association, Wheaton, IL 1964, revised).

Cully, Iris V., *New Life For Your Sunday School* (Hawthorn Books, Inc., New York, 1976).

Gangel, Kenneth O., *Leadership For Church Education* (Moody Press, Chicago, 1970).

Hyles, Jack, *The Hyles Sunday School Manual* (The Sword of the Lord Publishers, Murfreesboro, TN, 1969).

Schaal, John, *Superintendents and Leaders* (Baker Book House, Grand Rapids, MI, 1969).

Towns, Elmer L., *The Successful Sunday School and Teachers Guidebook* (Creation House, Carol Stream, IL, 1976).

October

S	M	T	W	T	F	S
					1	2
3	4	5	6	7	8	9
10	11	12	13	14	15	16
17	18	19	20	21	22	23
24	25	26	27	28	29	30
31						

28
Thursday

Chapts 4, ~~5, 6~~ 11

Meet Dec 1

September

S	M	T	W	T	F	S
				1	2	3	4
5	6	7	8	9	10	11
12	13	14	15	16	17	18
19	20	21	22	23	24	25
26	27	28	29	30		

November

S	M	T	W	T	F	S
	1	2	3	4	5	6
7	8	9	10	11	12	13
14	15	16	17	18	19	20
21	22	23	24	25	26	27
28	29	30				

Thursday, October 28, 1993

29 Friday
October
1993

Time	
7:00	
7:30	
8:00	
8:30	
9:00	
9:30	
10:00	
10:30	
11:00	
11:30	
12:00	
1:00	
1:30	
2:00	
2:30	
3:00	
3:30	
4:00	
4:30	
5:00	

4 The Reaching Arm of Sunday School

Anyone who properly teaches the Bible will be concerned about reaching lost people. The first part of the definition of Sunday School is found in the chapter title: Sunday School is the reaching arm of the church.

REACHING THE WORLD

1. God's desire for the multitude. In Deuteronomy 31:11,12, the Word of God tells plainly, "When all Israel is come to appear before the Lord . . . Gather the people together, men, and women, and children, and thy stranger. . . ." The truth of this command is repeated in the greatest verse in the New Testament, John 3:16: "For God so loved the world that he gave. . . ."

The gospel presents a picture of God's love for all people, so much so that Jesus gave Himself, not just for the saved but for the whole world (I John 2:2). Concerning the spiritual need of children to be saved, "Even so it is not the will of your Father which is in heaven, that one of these little ones shall perish" (Matthew 18:14). Therefore, the nature of God is tied to reaching the world.

2. Jesus' desire for the multitudes. Jesus proved His love by living in this world. "For the Son of man is come to seek and to save that which was lost" (Luke 19:10).

Again, Jesus said, ". . . for I am not come to call the righteous, but sinners to repentance" (Matthew 9:13).

A Sunday School teacher who has Jesus in his heart will manifest it by going after lost people who should be in his class. In Luke, chapter 15, there is the illustration of the woman seeking the lost coin and the shepherd seeking the lost sheep. These vividly portray the example of Jesus' love for the lost and how we should go after them.

3. The church's obligation for the multitude. The Great Commission commands, "Go ye therefore, and teach all nations" (Matthew 28:19a). Emphasis here is on the multitudes around the world. The early church fulfilled its command through Acts 5:42: "And daily in the temple, and in every house, they ceased not to teach and preach Jesus Christ." Later, Paul led the church in Ephesus in evangelism, "publickly, and from house to house" (Acts 20:20c). These are our examples.

Perhaps the verse that is applied most to Sunday School bus ministries is: "Go out into the highways and hedges, and compel them to come in, that my house may be filled" (Luke 14:23b). The Sunday School bus ministry has the Great Commission at its heart, going after the multitude.

As necessary as the bus ministry is, in some churches it has made Sunday School teachers lazy. When teachers rely on someone else to reach the lost, they become mere communicators of the Bible, hence losing their uniqueness. The task of reaching all people for Bible study is not optional; it is mandatory.

4. A vision for the multitudes. It is said you cannot achieve what you cannot conceive. Therefore, Sunday School leaders should have a vision of what they want to accomplish. Vision many times involves numerical goals. Recently a Sunday School advertised, "March to 500 in Sunday School during March." Its attendance had been 350 during the winter. It had a vision of reaching unsaved people and bringing them in to hear the gospel. A church in Baton Rouge, Louisiana, had a large motto in its auditorium: "Reach this city for Christ." Vision is necessary for growth. "Where there is no vision, the people perish" (Proverbs 29:18a).

Jesus had a vision of lost people, "But when he saw the multitudes, he was moved with compassion on them, because they fainted and were scattered abroad as sheep having no shepherd" (Matthew 9:36). These were not the people in the synagogues, nor under religious instruction; these were the multitudes. Sunday Schools die when they content themselves with those on their rolls. There is a future for the church with a burning desire to reach lost people through the Sunday School.

The multitudes are not in church buildings. Most of them are in shopping centers, office buildings, and suburbs. There are millions who have never been to Sunday School. Jesus tells us to lift up our eyes and look on the fields. A vision of unreached multitudes is necessary to move a church out into the highways and into the hedges.

5. A compassion for the multitudes. Vision leads to compassion. When Jesus saw the multitudes He was moved to compassion. This was not a casual stirring of emotions. This was a burden based on knowledge. To have a biblical vision, a Sunday School must see the multitudes as Jesus saw them. A Sunday School teacher will gain such a burden by spending time with the Lord in prayer.

But vision of the multitudes leads to generalizations if the vision does not include individuals. Jesus placed great value on the individual: "Ye are of more value than many sparrows" (Luke 12:7b). He also noted, ". . . joy shall be in heaven over one sinner that repenteth . . ." (Luke 15:7) and He "calleth his own sheep by name, and leadeth them out" (John 10:3b).

Sunday School teachers should develop the habit of praying for lost people individually. By developing a prayer list and becoming an intercessor, teachers begin to understand the value of a lost soul.

USING THE SUNDAY SCHOOL TO REACH PEOPLE

There are many Sunday Schools that are growing. The recent listing in *Christian Life* magazine of the 100 largest Sunday Schools proved there can be numerical growth in these days. They also listed the fastest growing Sunday School in each state in the United States, showing that all denominations, in all states, in all localities, can grow. There is no logical reason for a Sunday School not to grow, whether it be rural, inter-city, or an integrated Sunday School. The following are some steps to growth:

1. Find the prospects. One of the first steps in causing your Sunday School to grow is determining who should be in your Sunday School. A prospect is a person who *should* and *could* attend the Sunday School. Prospects can be found by the following methods:

(a) Search the Sunday School rolls for prospects. If accurate records are kept, people will be on the rolls who have not attended in quite awhile. Gather these people into a prospect list, especially noting the chronic absentees. Those who have dropped out over a period of time may be convinced to return. Perhaps at Promotion Sunday a pupil was lost because he did not like his new teacher. These are the prospects that should be the focus of attention.

(b) Use a buddy-search. Go through each Sunday School class and ask every member to give the names, addresses, and phone numbers of their friends. When prospects know members in a Sunday School, they are likely to attend, especially if they are contacted in the name of their friend. A buddy-search will reveal a number of prospects who could be in Sunday School.

(c) Take a religious census. Many Sunday School workers go throughout their neighborhood at least once a year, taking a religious census. This way they determine who is not attending church; these people then become prospects, and soulwinners can go after them. Other churches have found that this is not an effective means. Whatever is effective for you should be used.

(d) Use the Welcome Wagon list. Many neighborhoods print a list of new residents; this makes an excellent prospect list inasmuch as they are not settled into a church. Sometimes these people will respond to a friendly invitation to Sunday School.

2. Focus on the prospects. Make the reaching time and effort count. A Sunday School worker may go to a shopping center, inviting visitors to attend Sunday School, with small results. On a Saturday night, 2,000 leaflets might be passed out and not more than one or two visitors will come the following Sunday. If the Sunday School worker used the same amount of time and energy contacting definite prospects there would be a much higher percentage of visitors in attendance. Time spent contacting prospects is the most productive of all work in reaching the lost.

The following steps will help in reaching prospects:

(a) Pray for them. Perhaps the Sunday School class can pray for prospects by name. Or their names can be distributed so the pupils can take them home for intercession.

(b) Phone them. A teacher can distribute the names

and phone numbers of prospects to class members. When the pupils contact those of their own age, it is an effective way of reaching the lost.

(c) Write them. A postcard or letter can be mailed inviting prospects. If the class happens to print a newsletter, that will be effective, especially if it has a personalized note.

(d) Visit them. A strategy for visitation should be planned. Perhaps class members can visit the prospect, followed by a visit from the teacher, especially if there has been a phone call and letter to the home.

3. Provide an educational atmosphere. Many Sunday School rooms are drab and dreary. If you are planning on reaching the lost, make sure the room is inviting. It should say, "Come in!" Provide chairs and whatever other equipment, such as tables, etc., that is necessary for the age of the pupils meeting in the room. Seasonal decorations will be attractive, such as the bright colors of fall in October and November, or the new life of green trees and flowering bushes in the spring.

4. Provide space for growth. Space is needed to teach pupils the Word of God. When you have decided to reach the lost, there must be a place to teach them the Word of God. If your church has enough floor space, make sure it is divided properly among the classes. You may have to remodel your present building, or you may have to add a new building ultimately. Churches have been very innovative when it comes to adapting space. They have used offices, hallways, foyers, balconies, school buses, or the pastor's office. Homes in the neighborhood have been pressed into service as well as fire stations, funeral homes, empty store buildings, or public school buildings.

5. Meet visitors at the front door. Care should be taken to see that all who visit the church know how to get to their class. Someone should be in the foyer of the church to meet all visitors. Here the first-time attenders fill out a visitor's card and are directed to their classes. There should be ushers assigned to take or direct visitors to the classes. Someone should also be at the door of each department or class to welcome visitors and greet all who enter. Directional signs in the halls will keep visitors from becoming frustrated during the weeks they are still new.

6. Identify the rooms. The rooms should be marked with the name of the department or ages in the department and the name of the superintendent or teacher. Visitors are often fearful when first attending a Sunday School. When the room is clearly identified the visitor has a basis of relationship. He knows he belongs in the room with his peers. Knowing the name of the superintendent or teacher also helps the visitor to relate to him on a personal basis.

7. Maintain a regular soulwinning program. Growth for the sake of growth should never be the aim of a Sunday School. Emphasis should never be put on the result that is sought but on conditions that bring about the result. The condition to be sought in Sunday School is bringing souls to Christ; the result is a growing Sunday School.

The basis for soulwinning is scriptural. Therefore, an organized campaign is needed to help people involve themselves in reaching the lost. Harold Henniger, pastor of Canton Baptist Temple, noted, "Most Christians don't witness to their friends, but if they come to our church visitation program and go out on an assignment, they witness that evening. After the pump is primed, they begin voluntarily witnessing to their friends."

Plan a weekly soulwinning program for reaching the lost:

(a) Leaders set the example. The pastor, Sunday School superintendent, and all teachers must be present for visitation for it to be successful. They are examples to the rest of the Sunday School members. People encourage one another when they go out winning souls together. "For we are labourers together with God" (I Corinthians 3:9a).

(b) Set a definite time. When soulwinning is left to the convenience of people, they usually don't find the time. A specific time (or times) should be set and everyone urged to attend. Perhaps the ladies can visit in the morning and the men could go out in the evening. Some people need to be visited at different times of the day because of their work schedule. The bus workers should go visiting on Saturday morning.

(c) Make assignments. It is good for soulwinners to meet at the church before they go out. A short message and a time of prayer will equip them for their spiritual service. When they have prospects and absentees to visit, there is more purpose in their calling. Assignments make soulwinning urgent. When a soulwinner goes to the home, he should know whether he is going to obtain attendance, win someone to Christ, or follow up an absentee.

(d) Reports are necessary. After visits have been made, reports should be returned to the church. Workers are motivated when they compare their results with others. It helps to rejoice together when souls are saved, and to encourage one another when workers feel frustrated from a lack of results.

(e) Training soulwinners. Training sometimes requires weeks and months before people can become effective soulwinners. The fact that a person is a Christian does not guarantee that he knows how to lead someone else to Christ. Training classes are valuable, but on-the-job training is the most effective. Soulwinners should go out two by two. A young Christian going with a seasoned soulwinner can learn as much in one evening as he can by sitting through many classes.

PUBLICIZE FOR OUTREACH

The Sunday School must publicize its ministry to the community. This prepares the way for personal contacts. The following publicity can help reach lost people for Christ:

1. The pulpit. The pastor's support for Sunday School is absolutely mandatory. When the pastor pushes the Sunday School, the entire church becomes interested. When the pastor is not sold on the work of the Sunday School it will suffer. The pastor who makes Sunday School a special object in his home visits will note a response in increased attendance and offerings. The Sunday School's strength will add to that of the church.

2. Posters. When there are attendance campaigns, make sure that the church has posters in its halls, stairways, and on all bulletin boards. They will remind the church community of Sunday School outreach.

3. Flyers. Printed advertising should be delivered to the homes, passed out to attenders to distribute as well as for their own information, and mailed. It is important that the flyers reinforce what is happening in the Sunday School.

4. Newspaper advertisements. Ads for the newspaper should be both informative and interesting. Make sure they contain all the pertinent information of what, where, when, and perhaps why. Gear them to the unsaved person with a view of telling him what ministry your Sunday School performs. Don't overlook the opportunities of free newspaper advertising by submitting news items of Sunday School or church activities on a regular basis.

5. Church bulletins. Most everyone reads the church bulletin on Sunday. A short pithy comment about the importance of Sunday School will motivate some to attend. Don't forget to include statistics on growth and achievement. This will motivate others.

LEADER RESPONSIBILITY

The success of any outreach program depends upon the leadership: pastor, superintendent, and teachers. This is the order of responsibility in the church. Each week new prospects must be found, assignments made, and workers motivated to win souls. We cannot criticize a church when the people are not willing to reach their community. If a church is not winning souls, it is a leadership problem because everything rises and falls on leadership.

Leaders should keep the challenge of a growing Sunday School before all their workers. This challenge comes from:

1. Growing churches in the Word of God. The growing church we see in the Book of Acts reminds us that it is possible for today's churches to grow.

Then they that gladly received his word were baptized: and the same day there were added unto them about three thousand souls (Acts 2:41).

Howbeit many of them which heard the word believed; and the number of the men was about five thousand (Acts 4:4).

And daily in the temple, and in every house, they ceased not to teach and preach Jesus Christ (Acts 5:42).

And the word of God increased; and the number of the disciples multiplied in Jerusalem greatly; and a great company of the priests were obedient to the faith (Acts 6:7).

When we realize that such growth in the Jerusalem church was in spite of insurmountable odds and vicious opposition, we should be encouraged to be faithful regardless of problems that may be before us.

2. *The growth of other churches in our contemporary society.* Even though there are some dead churches these days, many churches are growing. If other churches have the blessing of God, why can't yours? Leaders will have to learn the principles of growing Sunday Schools and keep the vision of growth in front of their workers. Then they can grow.

SUMMARY

Soulwinning is the roof on the building, the ultimate step in God's plan. A Sunday School may have beautiful buildings, adequate visual aids, and enough equipment to get the job done, but it will fail without soulwinning. A Sunday School may have excellent teaching, but it will fail without soulwinning. A Sunday School may have plans, organizations, and programs, but it will fail without soulwinning.

All these other things are necessary, but soulwinning is the key that provides for the success of Sunday School growth. Unless regular, effective soulwinning is promoted, a Sunday School will not measure up to its highest possibilities.

GUIDE QUESTIONS FOR STUDY AND DISCUSSION

1. Give scriptural reasons for calling the Sunday School the "reaching arm of the church."
2. List several ways of finding Sunday School prospects.

3. What role does the atmosphere of the Sunday School play in reaching prospects?
4. How can a regular soulwinning program benefit a Christian?
5. Why should there be a definite time for soulwinning?
6. What is the most effective method of soulwinning training?
7. Name five ways to publicize your Sunday School.

ACTIVITIES FOR FURTHER STUDY AND APPLICATION

1. Have the class members share their burdens for Sunday School teaching. Then discuss how they can acquire a greater burden/desire for winning the lost to Christ.
2. Plan new ways for reaching prospects in your Sunday School.
3. Outline a plan of outreach/soulwinning for your Sunday School for a year.
4. Make a list of other techniques suggested in discussion for reaching people through the Sunday School that are not listed in this chapter.

RESOURCES

Barnette, N. M., *The Place of the Sunday School in Evangelism* (Convention Press, Nashville, TN, 1945).
Towns, Elmer L., *World's Largest Sunday School* (Thomas Nelson, Inc., Nashville, TN, 1974).

5 *The Teaching Arm of Sunday School*

The role of teaching was elevated when the title "Teacher" was constantly used to refer to Jesus Christ. The Gospels further emphasize its priority by placing the word teaching before preaching when referring to the ministry of Christ: "And Jesus went about all the cities and villages, teaching in their synagogues, and preaching the gospel of the kingdom, and healing every sickness and every disease among the people" (Matthew 9:35). Teaching was sowing the seed and preaching was reaping the harvest.

The greatest importance of teaching is seen when it was included in the Great Commission: "Go therefore and make disciples of all the nations . . . teaching them to observe all that I commanded you . . ." (Matthew 28:19-20, NASB).

Sunday School teaching is one of the greatest opportunities in the world to serve God. But with opportunity comes responsibility. Some people say that teachers are born and not made, but that is not true. Teaching involves laws, and those who apply the laws of learning can expect to accomplish results with pupils. Those who learn the principles of teaching can expect to become excellent teachers.

On the other hand, teaching is a gift from God (Ephesians 4:11). Therefore, teachers are given that capacity. A teacher of the Bible needs two sources of ability. He must be given the gift of teaching by God and he must develop his ability to teach; for teaching like every other gift from God must be encouraged. If God has given you an ability, He wants you to perfect that ability and become better at your calling.

Just because a teacher has the gift of teaching does not mean he will be suited for Sunday School teaching, however. Teaching Sunday School is different from most teaching. It involves a supernatural curriculum, the Bible; it involves a supernatural command, the Great Commission; it involves a supernatural notice and enduement, God's call and bestowal of gifts; it involves the supernatural power, the enlightenment of the Holy Spirit. Therefore, the teacher who teaches in Sunday School should be more than an instructor who teaches the Bible. He also has a responsibility for the spiritual welfare of his students.

SHEPHERDING RESPONSIBILITIES

The Sunday School teacher has the same responsibility to his class as the pastor has to his flock. Just as the pastor is the shepherd, so the Sunday School teacher must have a shepherd's heart. A Sunday School teacher is the extension of pastoral ministry into the life of the class.

Since a Sunday School teacher is equal to the pastor in responsibility but subservient in duty, an examination of the pastor's duty will reveal the definition of a Sunday School teacher. God's plan for the pastor is found in Acts 20:28: "Take heed therefore unto yourselves, and to all the flock, over the which the Holy Ghost hath made you overseers, to feed the church of God, which he hath purchased with his own blood."

God gives the pastor responsibility for every person

in his congregation; note the phrase "all the flock." Therefore, the pastor is responsible to teach every person in his church. But it is a physical impossibility for him to teach every person in a one-hour time span on Sunday morning. Also, it is improbable that he can adapt his lesson to small children as well as the young married couples and older adults. Therefore, he enlists the cooperation of Sunday School teachers in helping him perform the tasks. "And the things that thou hast heard of me among many witnesses, the same commit thou to faithful men, who shall be able to teach others also" (II Timothy 2:2).

The Sunday School teacher, like the pastor, has a threefold responsibility: (1) to lead the flock; (2) to feed the flock; and (3) to protect the flock.

1. A Sunday School teacher leads his flock. Paul commanded the elders at Ephesus to take heed to themselves and to the flock of which God had placed them as overseers (Acts 20:28). Leadership is not only giving commands; leadership involves example and dedication. The pastor and Sunday School teacher must live the godly lives that are required by the church.

Leadership also involves prayer and giving of oneself to the will of God. Leadership involves trying to win the lost to Jesus Christ, and motivating other people to follow Him. And it involves as well a concern for those who are absent from the teaching and preaching of Scripture. All of these are characteristics that should be found in pastors and Sunday School teachers.

Jesus said, "Ye shall *be* witnesses unto me" (Acts 1:8b, emphasis mine). God expects us to be a witness before we can give a witness. Therefore, God expects a teacher to be a leader before he instructs others.

2. A Sunday School teacher feeds his flock. God requires the pastor to feed all of the flock, but logistically he is not able to do it, especially in large churches.

Therefore, the teacher assists in this responsibility. The teacher is assigned an age responsibility to teach according to his gifts, desires, and burdens.

It is the teacher's responsibility to teach every pupil in his class the Word of God. He teaches by explanation, by questions, and by illustrations. He uses repetition, example, and visual aids. The Sunday School teacher uses every means possible to teach every pupil the Word of God that they may grow thereby (I Peter 2:2).

3. *A Sunday School teacher protects his flock.* Paul warned the pastors that grievous wolves would attempt to destroy the flock (Acts 20:29). In the same manner that a pastor should watch over his flock, a Sunday School teacher must protect his sheep from the influence of the world. This means visitation of absentees. If a young junior boy is absent for two weeks in a row, the teacher should mail a card, phone, and/or make a personal visit to the home. Some have the mistaken notion that visitation is an American advertising device to balloon attendance. Not so! Visitation is intended to protect straying lambs from the influence of the world. Even those physically ill need a protective call to reinforce their faith. The old adage is true: "A home-going Sunday School teacher makes a church-going pupil."

QUALIFICATIONS FOR SUNDAY SCHOOL TEACHERS

Every teacher will want to do the best job possible because the life of the teacher is the life of his lessons. Therefore, it is necessary that each candidate fit biblical qualifications.

1. *Being spiritual.* Obviously a teacher must have experienced the new birth and be assured in his own heart through the Word of God that he is born again

(John 1:12, 3:7; Philippians 1:6).

Next, a teacher must be sincere, dedicated and separated from the world. God commands, ". . . Be not conformed to this world" (Romans 12:2). The teacher should continually renew his mind so that he may do the perfect will of God, as this verse states. This is the spiritually-minded Christian who has assurance of salvation based on the Word of God (I John 5:11-13). Christ lives in the Christian and gives him strength to do all things, even to teach Sunday School (Ephesians 3:16-17; Philippians 4:13).

A teacher will want to set aside a certain time each day for prayer and meditation in order that he may grow spiritually. During this time, he will want to bring before God the names of each student in his class. This is his role as intercessor. Also, he should be reading the Word of God in a devotional manner in addition to the study of the Bible for his lessons.

A Sunday School teacher must be a consistent witness. His life, conversation, and actions must be consistent with his responsibility as a spiritual leader. His pupils will look up to him as an example. Every Christian sins (I John 1:8-10), but a teacher should not be content with his imperfections. He should strive for maturity so that he can say with Paul the apostle, ". . . be followers together of [with] me" (Philippians 3:17a).

The teacher should be faithful to the total church program—Sunday morning, Sunday evening, prayer meeting, and visitation services. He should enjoy the local church activities and seek the fellowship of other Christians. The broad yardstick for Sunday School teachers is that they glorify God as their chief motive in life.

As the teacher checks these qualifications, he will find himself falling short. Everyone, however, can improve his weak points by seeking to follow God's will.

2. *Being educationally prepared.* A Sunday School teacher who expects to be successful must be trained. Some have naturally grown into this position by watching teachers, both good and bad. But teacher training classes are the best way to prepare teachers. Here the teacher learns new methods of teaching, thus making his class more interesting and the lessons more meaningful. He learns to know the nature of pupils at their different ages, how to deal with problems in the lives of his pupils, and how to guide them into a better Christian life.

There is an old adage that states, "The child's mind is a fortress that cannot be taken by force or bombardment. His mind has a natural gate and there is an easy entrance to those who know how to find it." Therefore, a teacher must learn the nature of the pupils if he is to lead them into the Word of God. Some teachers fight with pupils while others are able to motivate pupils to seek righteousness. The difference? Some teachers understand the nature of their pupils while others do not.

In addition to specific training, a teacher should keep updated in his work by reading books dealing with his age pupils, and current articles in magazines on teaching techniques, methods, and new trends in Sunday School. This keeps the teacher stimulated with new ideas and encourages him to put forth his best.

The regular teachers meetings will also broaden his ability. Here he will pick up ideas, hints, or new techniques. The Board of Christian Education will provide special meetings and clinics to keep teachers up to date.

Local Christian education conventions and/or Sunday School conferences are excellent places to improve teaching techniques. Sunday School leaders should encourage all teachers to attend such conferences to strengthen their abilities.

3. *Being personally disciplined.* One of the strongest factors in the Sunday School class is the teacher's personality. A pupil once said, "It's not the way he teaches—it's the way he lives." Therefore, be careful that the teacher's life is consistent with his lesson plan. Only as life and lesson are in harmony will the class be effective.

Personality begins with a neat appearance and pleasing attitude. The teacher need not be dull and untidy, nor should he be grouchy and ill-tempered. On the contrary, he should be Christlike. "Let this mind be in you, which was also in Christ Jesus" (Philippians 2:5). When the pupils see Jesus Christ in their teacher, they will want to be like him.

Personality also involves a disciplined life. Followers look for predictability in their leaders, so teachers must be regular in attendance. The teacher must also be punctual. A tardy teacher will induce tardiness in the pupils. Above all, he should display the fruit of the Spirit: "love, joy, peace, longsuffering, gentleness, goodness, faith, meekness, temperance" (Galatians 5:22-23). This results in a vibrant, exuberant Christianity. Be careful about enthusiasm; it is contagious.

Remember, the teacher needs the ability to inspire those whom he teaches, and he can't unless he himself is inspired. The teacher who matter-of-factly presents the lesson with little enthusiasm will have a dead class. He must have a zest for living and a wholesome interest in life. Jesus said, "I am come that they might have life, and that they might have it more abundantly" (John 10:10).

AIMS IN TEACHING

Aims give Sunday School teachers direction in

instructing their classes. In a broad sense, teaching is meeting needs; therefore, a teacher is not teaching until the pupils have their questions answered. Hence, the prime and foremost aim of Sunday School teaching focuses on the spiritual needs of pupils. There are three sets of aims for meeting this need: (1) concerning the pupils; (2) concerning the curriculum; and (3) concerning the task.

Concerning the Pupil

1. To win every person in his class. The Great Commission has as its aim the winning of every person to Jesus Christ. Therefore, the Sunday School teacher should try to give as clear a presentation of the gospel as possible to as many as possible. He should saturate his class with prayer, commit himself to personal evangelism, and dedicate himself to visiting the lost.

2. To cause every pupil to grow spiritually. Conversion is a starting point in the Christian life. Then the pupils must grow in faith and knowledge. The path to maturity begins with Bible facts and moves on to understandings, appreciations, skills, and attitudes. The teacher should do everything possible to cause his pupils to grow spiritually.

3. To help his pupils evangelize others. No one can reach a lost person as can an acquaintance. Pupils will be more effective in winning their friends to Christ than the teacher. Recognizing this, the teacher will want to motivate his pupils to become soulwinners. He can do this by taking them soulwinning, instigating Sunday School growth campaigns, and praying for his pupils to be soulwinners.

Concerning the Curriculum

1. To teach the Bible as effectively as possible. The

teacher's aim is to get the Bible into the pupil and the pupil into the Word of God. This is called double transference. The curriculum is a planned aid for teaching the Bible in a systematic way, but remember, the Bible is the Sunday School Sourcebook. God has promised to bless His Word and that it will never return unto Him void. Teach the Bible.

2. *To make the best use of methods and curriculums.* Modern public schools have interesting teaching techniques. Their rooms are bright, colorful and geared to the students' interests. Educational television also has made learning fun and efficient in many respects. Therefore, the Sunday School teacher will have to devote himself to excellence in methods and materials to communicate the Word of God to contemporary pupils. These up-to-date educational techniques which challenge the Sunday School have not hurt education in God's house; they only challenge it to higher goals.

Concerning the Task

Many Sunday School teachers do not do an adequate job because they are ignorant of their responsibilities. The following outlines a job description for a Sunday School teacher. This is his task.

1. *To know your pupils.*

(a) Keep in mind that you are teaching people, not just lesson content. Know your class members individually. This involves contacts with them outside the class time as well as during class. Their needs both spiritually and physically will differ widely.

(b) Teach so as to meet the individual needs of all the class members. Apply the lesson truths, with wisdom, toward meeting the spiritual needs of individuals. Sometimes their physical, and even emotional needs, if not met, will be a hindrance to their spiritual growth. Try to really know each person.

2. To prepare adequately to teach the lesson.

(a) Pray for each pupil in the class that God may speak to his heart.

(b) Pray for wisdom in preparation, clarity in presentation, and sincerity in application.

(c) Start lesson preparation early in the week so Bible reading and experiences may be incorporated into your teaching.

(d) Read the Scripture and its background for several days. If possible read the Scripture lesson in several versions for clarification.

(e) Meditate on the passage by slow, thoughtful repetition of the Scriptures.

(f) Develop a central theme for your teaching. This is usually noted in your lesson manual.

(g) Study commentaries, Bible dictionaries, and a Bible atlas to obtain additional insight into the text.

(h) Develop a clear outline to guide in your teaching. From your teacher's manual choose the material that will fit your class needs and that which you want to emphasize.

(i) Arrange your class by learning activities, such as time for prayer, review, Bible study, memory work, puppets, handwork, or other activities suggested in the teacher's manual.

(j) Plan an interesting way to capture the pupils' attention and imagination. This may be an illustration, news event, visual aid, or question to stimulate thinking.

(k) Prepare the visual aids suggested by your curriculum, or plan stories, sword drills, discussions, buzz groups, dyads, or a flannelgraph you feel will help to get a point across.

(l) Know the work required in your pupil's book. Make sure that you can answer every question that he is asked to answer. Use this material in review, discussion and handwork.

(m) Write out several study questions to ask your class. These should answer the *who, what, when, where, why,* and *what does it mean* of the lesson. Don't wait until you get to class to make up questions or you will be caught between third base and home plate.

(n) Allow your pupils to ask questions. This open-ended approach to teaching lets the pupils feel comfortable with the subject.

(o) Suggest applications for the lesson; then let them make applications for themselves. Teaching a lesson without an application is like fishing without a hook.

(p) Know your lesson so thoroughly that you are not tied to your notes. Remember, *telling is not teaching; listening is not learning.*

(q) Be flexible. Because Sunday School teaching involves active pupils in living situations, you can never anticipate every eventuality. Therefore, be prepared.

3. To care for out-of-class duties.

(a) Prepare the room before the class arrives. Determine where you want the pupils to sit, what visual aids will be used and what decorations will enhance the lesson period. Maintain an attractive room at all times.

(b) Develop a file of resources. Here keep illustrations, outlines, poems, flannelgraphs, and visual aids that will help in future teaching. The visual aids you prepare for this year can probably be used again, with perhaps some improvements from insights you have gained, next time the lesson appears in the curriculum.

SUMMARY

The entire effectiveness of a Sunday School rests on its teachers. There can be curriculum, buildings, equipment, and organization, but it takes a human teacher to communicate to pupils. The quality of a Sunday School rises or falls on the teacher, his preparation, motivation, spirituality, and background.

Teaching is defined as guiding the learning experience of the pupils. This presupposes three qualities of teaching: first, the guide must have traveled the path; second, the teacher knows what experiences are necessary and how to cause them; and third, the teacher is pupil-related.

When the Sunday School teacher does his job properly, he is a shepherd to his flock. He is more than an instructor of biblical fact; he has a ministry from God.

GUIDE QUESTIONS FOR STUDY AND DISCUSSION

1. What two sources of ability does a teacher of the Bible need?
2. Name the threefold shepherding responsibilities of the Sunday School teacher.
3. What is the prime purpose of visiting absentees?
4. List three types of qualifications for the Sunday School teacher explaining why each is important.
5. What part does personality play in teaching?
6. Name three goals each teacher should strive for in each of his pupils' lives.
7. What role does the Bible play in curriculum?
8. Name three parts to the Sunday School teacher's task.

ACTIVITIES FOR FURTHER STUDY AND APPLICATION

1. List several creative ways you as a teacher can help

your students experience as well as hear Bible truths.
2. Develop a resource file (pictures, outlines, stories, poems, tapes, visual aids) that will help you in future teaching.

RESOURCES

Horne, Herman H., *Jesus, The Master Teacher* (Kregel Publications, Grand Rapids, MI, 1964).

Zuck, Roy B., *The Holy Spirit in Your Teaching* (Scripture Press Publications, Inc., Wheaton, IL, 1963).

6 Training Teachers for Sunday School

Is the successful Sunday School teacher born with the gift or made? Perhaps neither position is true, or both, depending on the individual. But there is no question at all that the most spiritually gifted teacher can be made better through training. A teacher can have ability, knowledge, and skills but these do not always constitute success. He will become a successful teacher as his desire to use his ability and knowledge grows. And teacher training deals with all these areas—desire, resources, skills and knowledge.

WHERE TO FIND TEACHERS

The first question is where to find good teachers. First, conduct a churchwide survey. Use a questionnaire to find those who have taught in the past, those who desire to teach, and what age group they desire to teach. Obviously many of those you find will not be trained, yet are qualified to teach Sunday School. Their desire to teach is a foundation on which they can be trained.

Vacation Bible School is another good source for potential teachers. Those who have helped during the summer might have received a burden to teach and now want to continue their task.

Sermons and dedication services for workers are

another good source for finding Sunday School teachers. Have the pastor preach a message on talents and their use. Then the pastor can give an invitation for those who feel called to teach to respond in a public service. Not everyone who responds is a good candidate for teacher training, but at least it shows a willingness to serve.

A nominating committee can be effective in some situations. This committee can make an objective evaluation of potential teachers in the church, then approach the person with a request to teach Sunday School and take further training.

After you have found a potential teacher, make a personal visit to discuss with him the task of teaching. This interview will give you needed background on the applicant. Also, it will help answer any questions he has on the task.

Before enrolling him in a training class, ask that he observe a class in operation. Of course, this observation is more than just watching. This observation time will make the actual teacher training class more beneficial.

AIMS FOR TEACHER TRAINING CLASSES

Teacher training is one of the paths to improving the quality of Sunday School. Training develops skills, improves techniques, and gives teachers access to new resources. Training classes give a systematic presentation of teacher aims, qualifications and duties. They also deal with attitudes and motivation. But the greatest advantage is that training classes give the teacher experience and confidence, the ingredients which produce learning.

There is no leading without reading. Unless the teacher is himself first a learner, he will have little to teach his pupils. Emphasizing the first law of teaching, the teacher must know more than he expects to teach. He cannot scrape the bottom of the barrel of his knowledge and be poised and enthusiastic at the same time. He must be able to dip into the "cream" on the top. That "cream" is his accumulated experience, partly gathered in training classes that prepare him to teach. While a teacher never stops improving in knowledge and skill, a basic course of training will provide the impetus for immediate and future efforts.

1. Better teachers. Obviously the purpose of a teacher training class is to have expert teachers. Since teaching is the guidance of learning, teacher training classes should have outstanding teachers who can lead the experiences that a future teacher needs. The best way to lead is by example of good classroom instructors.

There are many teachers already teaching who need polish and rejuvenation. Some mature teachers need the challenge of more teacher training. Because they have a superior background, they will learn at a deeper level than the novice.

Prospective teachers will be trained and ready when called to serve. The strong church will have a supply of qualified teachers that it can call upon. The only way to have this reservoir is to train all potential teachers who will accept the challenge.

2. Better learning. The purpose of the Sunday School is that people learn the Word of God. A good teacher training class will produce teachers who know the Bible because they have systematically studied it in a comprehensive program of teacher training. These teachers will elevate the entire level of learning in the church.

Thorough, knowledgeable teaching insures more learning at all levels. The teacher who knows the Bible will have confidence in the classroom. Hence he can give greater motivation for self-study of the Bible to his pupils.

The teacher's enthusiasm is contagious, therefore the greatest motivational tool that a teacher has is his own personality. It is said that minds speak to minds, feelings speak to feelings, and life speaks to life. The total life of the teacher (intellect, emotions and will) is communicated when he teaches the Word of God. The pupils' view of the Bible will become more exciting and alive because of the teacher's improved approach to teaching.

3. Better carryover. The teachers who have been through a teacher training class will have a better opportunity to apply the truths of the lesson because they understand the nature and methods of teaching/learning/application. As a result, the pupil will have more growth in grace through deeper understanding. Also, he will have a changed life through personal application of the truth.

4. Better enrollment and attendance. The church that has an effective teacher training class will improve its quality of education and, hence, will increase Sunday School enrollment, increase regular attendance (the barometer of interest) and will be able to begin new classes. Also, a side effect of teacher training is increased church attendance.

5. Better soulwinning. Good teacher training classes will produce better soulwinning on the part of the teacher and his pupils. The first reason is that more unsaved will be attracted and thus hear the good news. They will come because the class is exciting and thus can be reached with the gospel. Also, increased vision is another effect of teacher training. The teacher begins to see the need of the gospel everywhere. Finally, a more effective Sunday School class motivates members to have more zeal to reach the unchurched.

6. Better offerings. This is not the purpose of teacher

training but its result cannot be denied. More fully trained teachers will give larger offerings. Of course, a teacher should be tithing regularly before being asked to teach, but after training he will have a better knowledge of the work and will give more. Also, he can move his class to be more faithful to God.

WHERE TEACHERS ARE TRAINED

Some teachers excel at their profession and have never taken a training class, while some go through several classes and fail at every attempt. Obviously, there is more to training teachers than a training curriculum with structured classes.

1. Observation. Many teachers conduct their classes in methods similar to teachers that made a great impact on their lives. Either by observation or memory, the new teacher imitates someone else. So begin teacher training by observation. Have observation sheets available to guide the new teacher in recognizing important teaching factors. Indiscriminate viewing has little value although it might provide motivation and encouragement.

Observe both efficient and poor teaching. But be careful; poor teachers only instruct in what not to do. Learn positive lessons from good teachers.

2. Internship. Team teaching and the master teacher have brought a new, successful wrinkle to training. Teachers learn their role by assisting in the teaching process. There are many Christians who will help out in a class who will never assume the entire responsibility for the total lesson.

These assistants lead discussion groups, assist in handwork, present a part of the lesson or perform many other tasks. They are learning to teach by watching the master teacher and by actually teaching. As they participate in planning meetings, educational principles and techniques will "rub off" on them.

3. The Sunday School Library. Many consider the Sunday School library as simply a warehouse or collection of books for Christians to read. At one time this was the accepted practice of churches. Today, with inexpensive Christian paperbacks and the growing affluency of our society, almost all Christians purchase the books they read. As the traditional Sunday School library struggles to attract the average church member, a new ministry has emerged. Today, many feel the primary contribution of the Sunday School library is to the Sunday School teacher.

The Sunday School library purchases Bible encyclopedias, dictionaries, commentaries and other reference books that are beyond the financial reach of most teachers. Also, it provides visual aids, such as flannelgraphs, filmstrips, transparencies, films, and videotapes on Sunday School teacher training. Also, the Sunday School library could have a file of pictures, clippings, and illustrations in addition to audio cassettes.

The Sunday School library becomes a training center for both new and experienced teachers. The new teacher should learn how to use the Sunday School library to enrich his teaching. The librarian is a good friend who can help find illustrations, object lessons, and visual aids.

4. The Sunday School teachers meeting. This meeting brings together the Sunday School workers at regular intervals for study, fellowship, inspiration, problem-solving, planning, and business transactions. It is in the teachers meeting that: (1) problems are presented and considered; (2) solutions are sought; (3) new plans are discussed; (4) failures are faced and causes are discussed; (5) successes are reviewed; and (6) programs of action are formulated.

Both beginners and seasoned teachers grow through this meeting, so it becomes an integral part of training. Teachers become more proficient by faithful, sustained effort brought about by contact with fellow workers under conditions that motivate, enlarge vision, deepen responsibility, and strengthen loyalty.

A few churches still teach the coming Sunday's lesson at the weekly teachers meeting. But most provide teacher manuals; therefore, there is no need to inform teachers of the coming lesson. However, this is a good time for teachers in an open-class or department to coordinate their activities.

Teachers get a vision for the whole task of Sunday School at their teachers meeting. They realize they are not alone; they see their spoke in the wheel. Lack of cooperation by anyone weakens the whole.

5. Workers banquet. Prospective workers and regular teachers may be invited to a Sunday School banquet. The after-dinner program may be a couple of hours of training, discussion, and demonstration.

6. Saturday workshops. A Saturday afternoon (or a 10:00 a.m.—2:00 p.m. session, including potluck lunch) is a good time for a training session in the use of teaching techniques for all teachers and prospective teachers. An outside speaker can effectively demonstrate a variety of approaches to teaching. This should never be a "sit and listen" affair where the speaker merely lectures. It is more effective if it includes a demonstration and participation time, when workers are involved in learning by doing.

7. Conventions and conferences. Arrange for the church to sponsor new teachers as delegates to a statewide or national Sunday School convention where training in each age group is available. The importance of the work is magnified by the enthusiasm of large numbers of teachers dedicated to the same task.

8. *Evening school in local Bible colleges.* If you live near a Bible college check to see if it offers teacher training courses. These are usually evening courses, both credit and non-credit. Many Bible colleges are associated with The Evangelical Teacher Training Association and offer approved courses leading to credit. These may well supplement your local church's teacher training program.

SCHEDULED TRAINING CLASSES

All of the above suggestions are important in training teachers for the Sunday School; however, these are supplementary. A regularly-scheduled teachers training class should follow a specified curriculum and be required for all those who teach in the Sunday School.

This class is conducted at different times in various churches. Some meet during the Sunday School hour; others meet before the Sunday evening service during the training hour. Some meet on Wednesday before prayer meeting. Other churches have scheduled a course for five or six evenings in one week. Then again, seminars are growing in public acceptance. A two-day seminar could present twelve hours of instruction in Christian education on a weekend, Friday and Saturday.

While some books and correspondence courses are available for teachers who wish to pursue independent study, the Evangelical Teacher Training Association course provides lessons for group study that will lead all potential teachers through the basic training steps they need to equip them for their job. (See "Training Resources for Teachers" below.)

SUMMARY

The training program is usually initiated by an alert, progressive leader who will be responsible for all phases of the teachers' training. He will encourage teachers to attend conventions and provide for their doing so, calling for reports on the workshops when they return. He will schedule staff retreats and provide opportunities for apprentice teaching and training.

Successful training programs, once begun, should be held at regular times, within the time limits of the total Christian education program. A church may schedule the sessions for six consecutive evenings once a year, or twelve midweek meetings may be allotted for the purpose. Some churches use the course as an adult elective in Sunday School or during the evening training hour. Regardless of choice of time, it should be consistent for best results.

GUIDE QUESTIONS FOR STUDY AND DISCUSSION

1. How can potential teachers be recruited?
2. List the benefits of teacher training.
3. Discuss the various programs for training teachers.
4. What is the aim of a teacher training program?
5. How can a training program be started?

ACTIVITIES FOR FURTHER STUDY AND APPLICATION

1. Outline plans for a teacher training program in your church with suggestions for advertising and enlistment.

2. Prepare a special training program including in-service training that allows apprentice teaching.

RESOURCES

Chapman, Marie, *Successful Teaching Ideas* (Standard Publishing, Cincinnati, OH, 1975).

Hammack, Mary L., *How to Train the Sunday School Teacher* (Zondervan Publishing House, Grand Rapids, MI, 1961).

Milhouse, Paul W., *Enlisting and Developing Church Leaders* (Warner Press, Anderson, IN, 1946).

Towns, Elmer L. and Cyril J. Barber, *Successful Church Libraries* (Baker Book House, Grand Rapids, MI, 1971).

7 Establishing Standards for Sunday School

When a Sunday School is left to itself it will drift and become ineffective. Standards of excellence are needed to continually challenge every Sunday School to its ultimate potential. Sunday School standards provide an objective yardstick for measuring its progress or determining reasons why it is failing.

Just as an architect prepares blueprints to guide the workmen who construct the house, so a Sunday School needs its own blueprint so that all workers may judge their labor. God gave Moses a pattern for setting up the tabernacle in the wilderness. God also gave David a blueprint for building the temple at Jerusalem. The Sunday School needs standards, or a set of blueprints, for its growth. These are found in the Word of God. However, the exact principles and statistics are not written in the Bible as they are printed in Sunday School workbooks. Nevertheless, there are guiding principles.

The source of these standards is found in the Great Commission which contains the purpose of Sunday School. A Sunday School is the reaching, teaching, winning arm of the church. Out of this definition come the needs, aims, and program for Sunday School.

STEPS IN IMPROVING SUNDAY SCHOOL

The following steps can be applied to any Sunday

School, small or large:

1. Determine the standard. A standard should be established which presents what the Sunday School should be in all its areas. Among those who accept the Bible as the Word of God, most Sunday School standards are similar; however, there are minor differences from denomination to denomination. Printed at the end of this chapter is the standard distributed by the National Sunday School Association. Many of the points have been revised according to contemporary needs and it still stands as a good basic standard for measuring a Sunday School and its work. Study this set of criteria to determine a suitable standard for your Sunday School.

2. Locate the needs. After studying the criteria, watch for weakness in your program. Usually a committee (an appointed self-study committee or the Board of Christian Education) will study standards in light of performance to determine the educational needs of a church.

This may be a causal evaluation at the monthly meeting or an involved self-study program using a set of questionnaires. The most extensive questionnaire to evaluate the Sunday School is printed in the *Successful Sunday School and Teacher's Guidebook,* Elmer Towns (Creation House, Carol Stream, IL, 1976, pp. 353-89). There are eight sets of questionnaires, two for the entire Sunday School and one for each Sunday School department. These questionnaires will help to determine the exact point of weakness in the Sunday School. Since education is meeting needs, when the weaknesses are determined specific action can be planned.

3. Research the need. After a committee has determined the specific weaknesses in a Sunday School it should go to the table of contents in Sunday School books to determine resources concerning their problem. The members of the committee should study as carefully as possible principles, programs, methods, and materials that will solve their problems.

4. Determine the strengths. Filling out the questionnaires and examining the standards will also tell where a Sunday School is strongest. Since a leader always operates from his strengths, begin by finding the Sunday School's strengths; then work in areas where you can achieve the most help.

When a Sunday School staff examines its weaknesses, a spirit of pessimism usually sets in. By looking at strengths first the Sunday School staff can gain a sense of self-worth and make plans to improve its program out of a sense of achievement. No matter how poor, every Sunday School has achieved some level of ability.

5. Study the records. One of the best sources for evaluating a Sunday School is its past records. In the public school, records include punctuality, conduct, efforts, attitude, and grades in each subject. Periodic reports are sent to parents and guardians so that they may be informed of the child's progress. Only a few Sunday Schools keep and use a systematic record of their pupils. Most Sunday Schools keep only attendance; a few keep punctuality.

At one time, many churches used the six-point record system or some modification of it. The name of the system suggested the number of records kept on each student. The pupils were graded on six points—attendance, punctuality, bringing their Bible, offering, church attendance, and lesson preparation. This gave the teacher good criteria for the spiritual progress of each pupil.

6. Evaluate by observation. Someone should visit each of the classes in operation. Usually the superintendent or director of Christian education observes each teacher to determine his effectiveness. However, casual observation for the sake of watching a teacher is not always effective. Administrators need to be trained in what to observe. Criteria are needed to guide his observation so that he sees the total class. The observer should compare what he sees with the Sunday School standard; this way his suggestions have an objective basis. Otherwise, he may see only those things that irritate him or those things that meet his fancy.

7. *Strategy for improvement.* After a church has evaluated its strengths and weaknesses, it must determine a plan to carry out the Great Commission in its Jerusalem. This plan is based on the principles of Christian education that are reflected by the church's standard for success as found in the Bible.

SUNDAY SCHOOL STANDARDS

1. *Policies.* The Sunday School should have definite governing principles so that it may function efficiently and effectively:

• A Sunday School organized to teach Bible content.

• A Sunday School organized to change lives according to the New Testament concept.

• A Sunday School constituted to promote fellowship of believers one with another.

• A Sunday School administered to work in harmony with the Christian home.

• A Sunday School where people can administer their spiritual gifts.

• A Sunday School composed of teachers grounded in the Word of God and trained to meet the needs of individual pupils.

• A Sunday School designed to have an evangelistic thrust into the community.

• A Sunday School founded to nurture the spiritual

growth of teachers and staff.

- A Sunday School divided (by classes, departments, or age) to meet each pupil on his own age level.
- A Sunday School planned for expansion.
- A Sunday School informed concerning the denomination and ready to cooperate with it.
- A Sunday School established with a definite financial budget.

2. *Personnel.* The Sunday School shall have definite policy concerning the spiritual and academic standard of the personnel responsible for its ministry.

The Sunday School teacher should have the following qualifications;

- Personal salvation.
- The gift of teaching (Ephesians 4:11).
- A thorough knowledge of the Word of God (II Timothy 3:15-17).
- Daily devotions consisting of prayer and Bible study.
- Regular church attendance (Hebrews 10:25).
- Planning and administrative ability.
- Leadership qualities, the ability to inspire confidence.
- Vision, the ability to view the job objectively and not become discouraged in it (Philippians 3:13-14).
- Ability to express himself and communicate.
- A cheerful, radiant personality.
- A manifested love for children.
- Patience.
- The ability and desire to counsel.
- Originality, ability to create an interesting and diversified class session.

Duties of the teacher would include:

- Regularity in teaching the class.
- Visitation in the pupils' homes.
- Punctuality; be in class 15 minutes ahead of time.

- Attendance at Sunday School teachers meetings.
- Acquaintance with pupils through socials and other out-of-class gatherings.

3. Plan. The Sunday School shall have definite plans for the conversion and spiritual growth of the pupil. These plans are as follows:

- Salvation of every constituent Sunday School pupil.
    (1) Need of salvation.
    (2) Provision of salvation.
    (3) Acceptance of salvation.
    (4) Consequence of salvation:
        Dedication.
        Consecration.
- A systematic program to develop a full growth into Christian maturity.
    (1) Teach pupils to grow to maturity in Christ.
        Bible study
        Prayer
        Witnessing
        Memory work
    (2) Church membership.
        Instruction in church membership
        Baptism
        Reception of members
    (3) Church education.
        Sunday School administration
        Teacher training
        Personal evangelism
- Development of a social life that is honoring to the Lord.
    (1) Teacher-pupil relationship.
    (2) Participation in wholesome social activities.
- Develop a friendly relationship between the home and the Sunday School.

4. Progress. The Sunday School shall make definite

plans for expansion. Increased attendance, improvement of organization, and the addition of equipment shall all contribute to the salvation and spiritual progress of the student. To insure progress in the Sunday School, it must have the following:

• Teacher training for the new teacher and in-service training for regular teachers.

• Promotions each year for greater interest and incentive at all age levels.

• Evangelistic outreach within the Sunday School.

• Missionary education to broaden the vision of the total church.

• Prayer.

• A program to reach new families.

• Creation of new programs and departments as the Sunday School grows.

• A Board of Christian Education to guide the total educational program of the church.

• Training in the use of audiovisual aids.

• Extension work, such as a ministry to prisons or hospitals, mission work, youth groups, mission Sunday School and/or visitation.

5. Outreach. The Sunday School shall use varying methods of serving its students and reaching its community by means of visitation, advertisements and transportation.

• Well-organized visitation program.

• Follow-up program for absentees.

• Provide transportation (bus ministry) for those who desire to attend but have no means.

• A well-organized publicity campaign to make the church and community aware of the events of the Sunday School.

• Attention should be given to the total image of Sunday School in the minds of the public.

• Well-planned church calendar to coordinate

special events and meetings in the church.

6. Property. The Sunday School shall maintain adequate facilities and equipment for effectively housing and teaching its pupils.

• Twenty-five square feet per pupil or ten square feet of prime educational space per pupil.

• Strategic location in the center of its clientele.

• Separate classrooms for each class and separate rooms for departmental activities.

• Windows in each room, if possible.

• Adequate heating, lighting (natural if possible), ventilation (air conditioning).

• Cheerful, pleasant inner decor.

• Adequate washroom facilities, including facilities for younger children as well as adults; drinking fountains; all kept clean and well maintained.

• Nursery care department equipped with cribs, washable toys, baby bottle warmer, and separate washroom.

• Chairs, tables, shelves, pictures, bulletin boards for each age level adapted to the height of the children.

• Projectors, screens, flannel boards, chalkboards, record player, and other visual aids. A visual aid library could be combined with the church library.

• A church library with an adequate selection of books for Christian education and sections for books for all ages.

• Cloakroom space for each department.

• Piano available in every departmental area.

• Organized, labeled storage space for all equipment.

• Proper fire exits and equipment and instruction in using them.

• Kitchen facilities to provide for socials, programs or other needs.

• Sunday School office with sufficient space for

workers, records, filing system, and curriculum materials. Good office facilities aid administration.
- First aid kit available in Sunday School office.
- Wastepaper baskets in each room.

SUNDAY SCHOOL TEACHERS COVENANT

The employee who works for a living realizes that there are certain rules by which he must govern his actions. These rules usually set standards for his conduct, dress, and the way he performs his job. Because people are receiving wages, little is usually said about the agreement between employer and employee.

Such an agreement between a teacher and the Sunday School is called a Sunday School covenant, and gives guidelines to the teachers concerning their responsibilities. Teachers are asked to agree to the covenant at the beginning of their term of teaching. When teachers are appointed for life they should renew their covenant once a year by indicating agreement. Other Sunday Schools appoint their teachers for one year; then the covenant must be agreed to before any teacher is appointed for another term.

Administrators use different methods in asking teachers to give allegiance to the covenant. In some churches the covenant is printed and distributed to teachers. They must sign it at the beginning of the year. Other Sunday Schools post it on bulletin boards; there is a general understanding among the entire Sunday School that teachers live by the covenant. Still other Sunday Schools have a teachers dedication day.

A dedication day for teachers is recommended by most aggressive Sunday Schools. At the beginning of the Sunday School year all teachers are asked to come to the front during the church service. Each point of the covenant is presented by the pastor or Sunday School superintendent. Teachers are asked to give their verbal agreement; thereby, everyone in the congregation knows what is expected of a teacher. A public dedication places Sunday School teaching on the highest level of expectation. When pupils see their teachers pledge their devotion to the Sunday School covenant, they realize that Sunday School teaching is more than a haphazard responsibility.

Some Sunday School teachers covenants become very specific regarding the points of sin prohibited in the local church. Other Sunday Schools are broader because of their interpretation of Christian grace. Whatever the specific requirements by the church, they should be clearly defined in the covenant. The following covenant is printed to give Sunday School administrators a guideline in adopting a covenant for their specific use.

A Sample Teachers Covenant

Recognizing the high privilege that is mine to serve my Lord through our Sunday School, and trusting in the help and guidance of the Holy Spirit, I earnestly pledge myself to this covenant.

1. I will live what I teach about separation from the world and purity of life, abstaining from all appearance of evil, setting an example in dress, conversation, deportment, and prayer (I Thessalonians 5:22).

2. I will be faithful in attendance and make it a practice to be present early to welcome each pupil as he arrives. If at any time, through sickness or other emergency, I am unable to teach my class I will notify my superintendent at the earliest possible moment (I Corinthians 4:2).

3. I will at all times manifest a deep spiritual concern for the members of my class. My first desire shall be to bring about the salvation of each pupil who does not know the Lord Jesus and to encourage the spiritual growth of every Christian (II Timothy 2:2).

4. I will carefully prepare my lessons and make each lesson a matter of earnest prayer (I Thessalonians 5:17).

5. I will regularly attend and urge all members of my class to be present at the church services, recognizing that the church and Sunday School are inseparable. Believing in the importance of prayer, I will endeavor to maintain regular attendance at the midweek prayer service as well as Sunday services.

6. I will teach according to the doctrines of our church, Christ our Saviour, Sanctifier, and Coming King (Acts 20:27).

7. I will wholeheartedly cooperate with the absentee program of our school and will strive to visit the home of each pupil at least once a year (Matthew 18:12).

8. I will heartily support the Sunday School program, attending the teachers meetings and the training classes (II Timothy 2:15).

9. I understand that my appointment as a teacher is for the 12-month period beginning the first Sunday of the Sunday School year. Whether my appointment is made then or later in the Sunday School year, I understand that it automatically terminates with the last Sunday of the Sunday School year and that decisions regarding re-appointment are based on my fulfillment of this teachers covenant (I Corinthians 3:9).

10. I will cheerfully abide by the decisions of my church and Sunday School, cooperating with my fellow workers in bringing our work to the highest possible degree of efficiency as one of the teaching agencies of the church (Matthew 28:19, 20; John 15:16).

SUMMARY

Just as everything in life will rust or decay without attention, the Sunday School will deteriorate without standards. There must be a written set of criteria for the total Sunday School and an objective covenant for teachers; otherwise, the quality of the Sunday School will suffer because administrators and teachers will rely on their feelings to carry out their joy. The Sunday School that keeps its standards polished will have a clear vision of the future.

GUIDE QUESTIONS FOR STUDY AND DISCUSSION

1. Why are Sunday School standards needed?
2. What should be the source for Sunday School standards?
3. What are the seven steps for improving a Sunday School?
4. What is one of the best sources for evaluating a Sunday School?
5. List the qualifications for a Sunday School teacher.
6. What plans should a Sunday School have for its pupils?
7. What are some of the necessary ingredients for progress in the Sunday School?

8. Name several methods of Sunday School outreach.
9. What items should be covered in the teachers covenant?
10. What are the advantages of a Teacher Dedication Day?

RESOURCES

Hakes, J. Edward, *An Introduction to Evangelical Christian Education* (Moody Press, Chicago, 1964).

Towns, Elmer L., *The Successful Sunday School and Teachers Guidebook* (Creation House, Carol Stream, IL, 1976).

8 The Sunday School Curriculum

While many factors influence success in a Sunday School, the two most important ingredients in a workable formula are: (1) the trained, dedicated teacher; and (2) an effective, Bible-centered curriculum. These two forces combine to create a Sunday School of high academic standards. Spirit-guided, it will effect learning in all its life-changing ramifications.

THE CURRICULUM

1. Definition and function. The word *curriculum* comes from a term that means racetrack. It was the course that guided the runner to the goal. Technically, a curriculum is a course of study that is organized to guide the pupil to specific objectives by the proper use of content, experience, teaching aids, teacher influence, application, and motivation. Therefore, a curriculum in Sunday School is a course of study of the Bible and related subjects which leads to and accomplishes the Great Commission.

Curriculum must be planned and comprehensive. It is planned to meet the needs of each age group of the Sunday School and comprehensive enough to provide study of all the Bible. Curriculum is not the purpose of the Sunday School; it is the means to accomplish the purpose. In most churches, that means that the curriculum will provide the means of leading pupils to the saving knowledge of Christ and then guide the teacher in instructing pupils to grow in character, service, and witness.

2. *Curriculum materials.* The term *curriculum materials* includes the books and aids which carry the curriculum into the learning experience of the pupil. This would include the items usually listed on the publisher's order blank used by Sunday School departments: teacher's book; pupil's book; and teaching visuals, such as charts, filmstrips, pictures, memory work games, puppets, and other items.

The curriculum materials should provide good variety in teaching methods, learning activities and pupil experiences suitable for each age. They will aim for outreach into the various areas of pupil life, including home, school, church, and recreation.

TYPES OF CURRICULUM

There are different kinds of curriculum materials with various methods of covering Bible content. The "Modern Curriculum Plans" chart shows the four chief kinds of curriculum plans and their relative values. If a pupil lived within walking distance of four different churches, he might encounter four different series of lessons in his own age group if he visited the churches on successive Sundays. This is one of the most effective arguments for a pupil's regular attendance at the same Sunday School. When a pupil skips from one Sunday School to another, he gets a smattering of unrelated biblical knowledge because of different curriculum plans (or possible lack of plans) used.

This is also an effective argument for a Sunday

Modern Curriculum Plans

UNIFORM GRADING	UNIFIED GRADING	DEPARTMENT GRADING	CLOSE GRADING
The same Bible portion is taught to each age-group.	Different Bible content, related by a single theme, is taught to each age-group.	Different Bible content is provided for each department group (Primary, Junior, etc.).	Different Bible content is provided for pupils in each public school grade.
(1) A small church can unite all pupils in a single lesson-related worship service. (2) All family members can discuss their common lesson at home.	(1) Several age-groups can meet in a single theme-related worship service. (2) At-home discussion of the theme is possible.	(1) All activities are closely related to the Bible lesson in each department group. (2) Lessons can be geared to the social, psychological, emotional and mental level of all pupils.	(1) Curriculum can be planned to fit the stage of development of pupils.
(1) Lessons are repeated on a 5-7 year cycle, provide limited Bible coverage. (2) Bible content often not suitable for pupils of all ages.	(1) Limited number of themes make it difficult to give complete Bible coverage. (2) Lessons taught in each department determined by theme, rather than pupils' developing needs.	(1) Common at-home discussion is limited, since parents and children study different material.	(1) At-home discussion limited. (2) Hard to relate all activities in SS hour (songs, worship service, etc.) to theme, since each grade has a different lesson.

Here are the four basic plans evangelical publishers follow in grading their lesson materials. To evaluate curriculum, you need to study the advantages and disadvantages of each curriculum plan when applied to your needs and goals.

From The Successful Sunday School and Teacher Guidebook, Elmer Towns, Creation House. Used with permission.

School to adopt one specific curriculum and require it to be used throughout the Sunday School. The confusion is obvious if teachers were allowed to choose courses from various curriculums. Individual teachers might be satisfied with the chosen lessons, but in the long run the pupils would suffer. They would not be receiving lessons based upon Bible knowledge learned in earlier grades. This usually results in great gaps in learning, or overlapping of some areas of Bible teaching.

The chart affords analysis and evaluation; it does not attempt to promote one plan in preference to others. However, it does show the comparative advantages and disadvantages of these plans. These must be taken into consideration and carefully followed in evaluating materials to be chosen.

1. Uniform grading. Publishers and constituents of the *uniform-grading* curriculum maintain that it unifies the family because everyone has the same emphasis at Sunday School. More opportunity is available for united Bible study in the home. With the same basic lesson their interest is mutual. Such lessons are often limited in scope because all age groups must cover the same material. The material is usually adapted to the various younger age groups leaving much of the Bible not studied by young people and adults.

2. Unified grading. The *unified-grading* curriculum has a central theme for the whole Sunday School; each class may have different Bible content. Its strength is the unity it gives to the family and church. It has the same weaknesses as the uniform grading curriculum.

3. Department grading. The size of a Sunday School will often dictate which of the four plans is most feasible. The *departmentally-graded* material is sometimes considered best suited for Sunday Schools with 150 to 400 in attendance.

4. Close grading. Sunday Schools over 400 can

better adapt *closely-graded* materials into their program. Of course, any of the curriculums can be adapted to any size Sunday School.

"I didn't closely-grade them—God did," one outstanding Christian educator said. Because younger pupils are progressing in grasp of knowledge and in understanding each year, their needs may be best met with closely-graded (age-graded) materials which keep up with their development year by year throughout the elementary grade years. The youth departments could study in a departmentally-graded way. The "Grading According to Need" chart shows how one curriculum accomplishes this. It also allows smaller Sunday Schools to use closely-graded materials from the beginning while they are growing large enough to become fully graded.

The "A" column shows how each age or grade during the elementary years is taught separately when there are enough students and teachers, and space is available. For fewer students, teachers or space, the "B" column shows how closely-graded material can be cycled on a two year basis; two grades are combined while the remaining grade meets alone. (Notice that it is important when using this method that the first grade meets alone because of their greater need for reading help and the sixth grade meets alone because of the greater advancement of these pupils over the rest of the Junior Department.) Column "C" shows how, for even smaller churches, pupils are combined into a department and the closely-graded material is rotated.

The chart also shows how the youth departments and adults meet departmentally or by classes for social purposes, and all in the same department study the same course. Each youth department cycles twelve courses and the adult department cycles forty courses so none need be repeated in ten years of study.

Grading According to Need

				SUNDAY SCHOOL		
			AGE	A	B	C
Closely Graded Courses	Preschool	Bible Beginnings	2	Courses for 2's	Rotate courses for 2's & 3's on a 2 year cycle	Use Kindergarten courses adapting for younger children
			3	Courses for 3's		
	Kindergarten		4	Courses for 4's	Rotate courses for 4's & 5's on a 2 year cycle	
			5	Courses for 5's		
			GRADE	A	B	C
	Primary Department	Bible Theology	1	Courses for 1st grade	Courses for 1st grade	Rotate courses for 1st, 2nd & 3rd grades on a 3 year cycle
			2	Courses for 2nd grade	Rotate courses for 2nd & 3rd grades on a 2 year cycle	
			3	Courses for 3rd grade		
	Junior Department	Bible Survey	4	Courses for 4th grade	Rotate courses for 4th & 5th grades on a 2 year cycle	Rotate courses for 4th, 5th & 6th grades on a 3 year cycle
			5	Courses for 5th grade		
			6	Courses for 6th grade	Courses for 6th grade	
Departmentally Graded	Junior High	Bible Establishing	7 8 9	Three Year Course—Junior High's can meet in one class or in 3 separate classes—all will study the same course		
	High School	Bible Equipping	10 11 12	Three Year Course—High Schoolers can meet in one class or in 3 separate classes—all will study the same topics		
	Adults	Bible Exposition	Adult College Career	Ten Year Course—Different course every Quarter for 10 years, then cycle is repeated		

From Accent on Life Bible Curriculum, Accent-B/P Publications, Denver

CURRICULUM PLANNING FOR ADULTS

Youth and adults who have been regular in Sunday School throughout their lives may tend to feel the lessons have no relevance to them now. They've "heard all that." In choosing curriculum for them, leaders should bear in mind that these students need materials which apply Scripture truth to their specific needs and problems. They need lessons that will challenge them to dedication of life in service to the Lord and His church. The following are some possibilities.

1. Bible study courses. A number of publishers offer study courses which cover books of the Bible or the whole Bible. These have study questions for students to research the purpose of a particular passage and its meaning for their lives. Such study accomplishes more than implanting factual knowledge; it also makes application and effects change—which adds up to real learning.

Bible study without an objective is as effective as shooting at a target without taking aim. "Aim at nothing, and you're sure to hit it," one phrased it. While all Sunday School teachers should teach from the open Bible and pupils should study with its pages open, lesson guides are necessary for both teacher and pupils to completely cover the Scripture in a systematic manner.

2. Elective courses. In addition to Bible study, per se, there are several areas of study that adults need and enjoy. These topics may cover evangelism, church history, world religions, cults, archaeology, Bible backgrounds, Christian ethics, the Christian family, and a number of other vital issues.

Some Sunday Schools allow adults, including the college/career young adults, to select one of several courses offered on current topics. Or a class may vote on its next topic of study; hence, the class elects its curriculum. Ideally, the books studied contain twelve chapters or can otherwise be adapted to last three months. Since interest preceded learning, an elective approach often does much to change lives.

3. Leadership training courses. It is a wise practice for a Sunday School to maintain one class continually offering a course in the Evangelical Teacher Training Association's training program. It provides an opportunity for strengthening the present leadership of the church available during the Sunday School period, and also trains prospective leaders. Sunday School teachers might be relieved of their duties for a quarter at a time to take refresher studies in this class.

In this program adults are trained to study the Bible independently and to be able to share their knowledge with others. They are taught understanding of the various age groups and how to evaluate their effectiveness with a particular group.

Other special class opportunities would be a new converts class, or brief class units might be taught on special topics, such as how to be a better usher, department superintendent, secretary/treasurer, or for other areas of service in the church.

CURRICULUM EMPHASIS

The curriculum of Sunday School begins and ends with God's revelation to men as found in the Bible. This is both a natural and supernatural book, so both natural and supernatural factors must be considered in teaching (I Corinthians 3:9). Human men wrote the Bible using the language of their day. Therefore, human teachers must communicate the Bible in the context of our time (Matthew 28:10; II Timothy 2:2). But God's Spirit wrote the Bible by divine inspiration, guiding every word to its exact place (I Timothy 3:16; I Corinthians 2:10-13). Therefore, the Holy Spirit must be active in the teacher process (John 14:26). This is accomplished by the following emphasis:

1. Christ-centered. The basic curriculum of the early church was Christ; He is still the core of Christianity. Sunday School must present the historical truth of Jesus Christ: His life, ministry, miracles, death, resurrection, and ascension into Heaven. But students must also be brought into a personal experience with Christ; He must live in their lives by faith (Ephesians 3:17).

2. Bible-grounded. If you teach Christ apart from the authority of the Bible you will probably drift into heresy or emotionalism. The objective basis of our faith is grounded in the Word of God. A Christian cannot grow in Christ without knowing the Bible; therefore, our Sunday School curriculum must include Bible facts and content.

3. Pupil-related. The ministry of Christ was person-centered. He continually related to the needs of those around Him. The Bible lesson must begin with the needs of our pupils and end at meeting those needs. The Word of God cannot be taught in a vacuum. The Great Commission demands, "teaching them to observe"; the student must practice the Bible.

CURRICULUM EVALUATION

It is obvious that a great deal of informative study and prayerful consideration must go into the choosing of a curriculum for the Sunday School. The Board of Christian Education should have the responsibility of choosing the curriculum, where such a board exists. If there is none, the pastor and the Sunday School superintendent may make the decision. It may be done after the Sunday School superintendent meets with the department superintendents, or in smaller churches, with individual teachers.

The evaluators should examine several sets of curriculum materials within the church's theological emphasis. While most denominations have their own publishing houses and their own curriculum materials, some churches may want to use literature from an interdenominational or independent publisher for a different approach to teaching or a different emphasis.

There must be criteria for deciding which materials should be adopted for regular use in the Sunday School. Some curriculums may be theologically sound, yet not meet the personal needs of pupils. The next curriculum may be denominationally geared, for a specific denomination other than your own. Some materials may be too expensive for the financial budget of the church.

Some of the criteria for making this crucial decision are as follows:

1. Theological content. It is the responsibility of the evaluator to test the curriculum's doctrinal agreement with the church's doctrinal statement.

2. Lesson content.

• Are the lessons correlated with a total curriculum plan? Do they build upon previous lessons?

• Are the materials properly age-graded?

• Is the teacher's guide adapted to the aim, experience, and needs of the class?

• Is the pupil's guide likewise adapted and interesting?

• Will the planned lessons lead to decisions for salvation, spiritual growth, and Christian service?

3. Appearance.

• Are the materials attractive?

• Does the format of the books appeal to teachers and pupils?

- Are pictures contemporary and colorful?
- Are the materials durable?

4. Teacher's helps.

- Is there an outline or general guide for aid in preparation?
- Are necessary materials listed for quick reference?
- Is a definite lesson application made?
- Do teaching resources encourage the use of the most effective variety of teaching materials, as opposed to the monotony of the same approach for every study?
- Are there suggestions for displays and illustrations?
- Is provision made for emphasis of special days, such as Easter, Christmas, Thanksgiving, Mother's Day, and Father's Day?
- Do the stories include character-building as well as Bible facts?
- Do the lessons challenge dedication of life on the part of the pupil?

5. Pupil's helps.

- Is adequate learning material provided for pupils, such as pupil books, activity sheets, take-home papers?
- Does the written work encourage active Bible study?
- Do learning assignments challenge the pupil's interest and knowledge?
- Do the paperwork assignments relate to the pupil's experience and age level?
- Are illustrations authentic and pertinent?

Evaluators of Sunday School curriculums may find that no one curriculum provides all the above desirable features. Aim toward choosing the curriculum that gives the best balance of Bible content, learning activities, and application of truths to life.

SUMMARY

The Sunday School curriculum is the foundation on which the Sunday School is built. Therefore, the curriculum must be supernatural in scope, spiritual in emphasis, yet practical in result. The curriculum must give a complete, systematic, comprehensive coverage of Bible content and apply the lessons to the lives of the pupils.

GUIDE QUESTIONS FOR STUDY AND DISCUSSION

1. What is *curriculum*?
2. What is the purpose of curriculum?
3. List the four well-known types of curriculums.
4. What factors should be considered in planning for adults?
5. Name three important areas that should be emphasized in a Sunday School curriculum.
6. Who should be responsible for choosing curriculum and curriculum materials?
7. What are the basic criteria for evaluating curriculum materials?

ACTIVITIES FOR FURTHER STUDY AND APPLICATION

1. Compare your church's present curriculum with the "Modern Curriculums Plan" chart. Into which category does it fit? What are the results, as you see them?
2. Order sample curriculum materials from at least three publishers. Evaluate them according to what you

have learned in this chapter.

RESOURCES

Mayes, Howard and James Long, *Can I Help It If They Don't Learn?* (Victor Books, Wheaton, IL, 1977).

Reisinger, D. K. and C. A. Risley, *Teach With Confidence* (Evangelical Teachers Training Association, Wheaton, IL, 1965).

Richards, Lawrence O., *A Theology of Christian Education* (Zondervan Publishing House, Grand Rapids, MI, 1975).

Towns, Elmer, *The Successful Sunday School and Teachers Guidebook* (Creation House, Carol Stream, IL, 1976).

Zuck, Roy B. and Robert E. Clark, *Childhood Education in the Church* (Moody Press, Chicago, 1975).

9 Methods of Teaching

The importance of Sunday School teaching lies in its definition. *Teaching in Sunday School is guiding the learning of pupils with the ultimate purpose that the gospel will change the lives of its hearers.* Obviously, teaching is much greater than just presenting truth. It is a process that involves the teacher and pupil with the Word of God. Therefore, it is imperative that Sunday School properly teach the Scriptures if it is going to grow according to New Testament standards.

TEACHING BY EXPLAINING THE WORD OF GOD

The Scripture is the Word of God which is the source of the Christian life. In Sunday School, the teacher should use as many methods as possible, but the foundation of instruction is explaining the text of the Bible.

The Word of God gives a foundation of doctrine (II Timothy 3:16); it cleanses the life (Psalm 119:9, 11); it gives power (Matthew 4:6-9); it comforts (Jeremiah 15:16); it gives direction for living (Psalm 119:105); and is the source of eternal life.

There is a special place for teaching the Word of God to the unsaved. The Bible will convict them of sin

(Jeremiah 23:29); it will point them to Jesus Christ (John 1:36); it will give them a new nature (II Peter 1:4); and will be the instrument that causes them to be born again (John 1:12; I Peter 1:23). Therefore, explaining Scripture is the foundation of Sunday School.

1. Teacher's presentation. There are many methods of teaching, but at the heart of the process is a presentation by the teacher. This is usually called the *lecture method* and is the foundation of instruction in explaining the text of the Bible.

The teacher must be well-equipped when he attempts to explain the Word of God. He must have an overall view of the subject and its relationship to the life of the pupils. In class he must not come across as dogmatic or "pushy." Yet the teacher should know what he believes and be able to explain it to his class. The teacher is a shepherd; he must lead the sheep to green pastures where they may feed upon the Word of God.

The spoken word has strong impact upon young minds. This is why Moses, Paul, and other great leaders of God have made use of speaking the Word of God. Yet, none of them limited themselves to lecture alone. There are times when the teacher will want to lecture because (1) it saves time, (2) he can cover more ground, (3) he can handle larger groups, or (4) it is the easiest method to use.

2. Pupils' involvement. The success of the teacher's presentation depends upon the teacher. If he is dominant, the class will not be included in the learning process. If he is vague and non-directive, the class will not know where it is going. It is important in the teaching-learning process that the teacher guide the students into the aim of the lesson by *personal involvement.* There should be a balanced approach.

When the teacher chooses to present the lesson by the lecture method, he will keep better attention and gain greater results if he supplements the lecture with involvement. After developing a point in the lesson he can stop and ask a question and wait for volunteers to answer it. This will likely lead to discussion as another question is asked and the answers are drawn from the students. Other methods of teaching may be used for a brief time—brainstorming, role playing—to amplify a point; then the teacher can return to the next point in the lecture.

TEACHING BY USING ACTIVITIES

Children are eager to learn. Their active, growing bodies need opportunity to move and explore the classroom. Children need to be able to walk about the classroom. They should feel the freedom to ask questions about what they see.

Movement in and of itself, however, is not enough. A Sunday School must provide ways for preschoolers to explore the lessons they are learning. Elementary students need to use their hands and feet for involvement. Older students use their minds to interact with one another.

Children are not good sitters, nor are they good listeners, but they are excellent learners. They like to learn from books, pictures, and posters on the wall. They like to learn by asking questions and they like to learn by seeing different things. Because children are dynamic growing personalities, they learn "beefstew" style. They learn many lessons at the same time. They acquire skills, memorize verses, imitate the teacher's life, and learn how to get along with other children. All these lessons come in one learning process.

Sometimes the active involvement of children makes adults uncomfortable. They want the pupils to sit still and be quiet, but the little ones are not made that way. Of course, there should be a time and place during the session for them to sit still and listen as the teacher explains the Bible. However, organized informal learning takes place all during the session through the children's activities.

1. Learning activities. For the younger children various areas may be set up where certain activities are centered. Prepare a circle of chairs or large rug for a story time. Tables should be provided for handwork, such as coloring, cutting and pasting, with shelves nearby to hold the supplies of crayons, papers, pencils, paste, etc. Also, a table is needed that would hold a nature display—plants, goldfish bowl with fish or sand and seashells, or a treasure a pupil brought back from a vacation trip and is loaning to the class for a while. A memory center will provide space for the memory chart and related materials. Books and games center will allow a child who has finished his work ahead of others to go and involve himself in looking at a book, working a puzzle, or enjoying a game, all of which have previously been presented in a teaching session. Many other possibilities will come to the mind of a creative teacher.

Never forget that children learn by doing—by coloring, pasting, growing a plant, or drawing a mural on the wall. Elementary school children learn by searching the Bible, talking to one another or by planning group activities. They also like to ask their teachers questions. As they open up in discussion, it is an indication they are opening their tender hearts to God.

Remember that the walls of a department or classroom teach, also. Teachers can speak to their pupils by what they place on the walls—posters, verses, murals, calendars, and seasonal decorations. A teacher can give himself a simple test. Walk through the classroom and ask the following questions: Is this room attractive? Is there something fresh in the room that was not there last month? Are there attractive pictures on the wall? A display? Something from nature? Are illustrations of the children's handwork on display?

Informal learning happens best when there is formal preparation. This takes leadership on the part of the teacher.

2. *Appealing to interests.* Children are interested in just about everything in life, but each age level has its own attractions and fascinations. The teacher can instruct through the interests of the pupils.

Small children love animals, nature, gadgets, colors, object lessons and flowers. As they get older, they are more interested in getting along with one another and the world beyond their home. As they move through their teen years, once again their interests expand into the world in which they live—vocation, marriage and love. Finally, adults are concerned about having a family, relating with their mate, and solving the vocational problems of their life.

The Bible speaks to every need in life. People are interested in living a happy, meaningful life; therefore, pupils can be reached through their interests. The teacher who is always telling his pupils to "sit still and listen" is ignoring the fact that God built desires into them. Pupils want to learn, move and ask questions. Life is active and teaching must be conducted in the active tense.

TEACHING BY MEETING NEEDS

Involvement for the sake of involvement can become just "busy work." Listening to a lecture may just be "routine." Also, coloring or pasting may become unexciting. A teacher can go through all the motions of teaching, but until he has met his students' needs, he has not taught the lesson. Facts about the Bible and words from the manual may be quickly forgotten, but when the Bible meets the needs of the pupil, the lesson will stick to his life.

The teacher who meets needs has to deal with the rapid learner who explores much more than the child who is rebellious. The teacher who meets needs tries to motivate the pupil who is uninterested. The teacher needs to know his pupils in order to help all of them.

The purpose of the Sunday School is spiritual growth. Children grow as their inner problems are solved and their needs met. Teaching a baby how to walk illustrates this point. We do not lecture to him on the principles of walking. Nor do we give him a demonstration of how to walk. Watch how a father teaches his child to walk. He takes the baby by both hands, holding and guiding his every action. Sometimes the father will tenderly pull the left hand forward, causing the baby's left foot to take a step. Then he repeats the process with the right hand. The ultimate aim is that the child may walk without the help of the father.

Sunday School is helping pupils walk in the Lord. Teachers can be most effective when they work with individuals helping them take one step at a time. Suppose the child took his first step and the father was disappointed because he did not run. The father's disappointment could destroy the initiative of his son. When pupils take a spiritual step, the teacher should show them love and support in every step. A sense of achievement and direction is part of learning; the teacher must give this to pupils.

TEACHING BY IMITATION

The teacher determines what learning will go on in

the classroom. The teacher who loves the Word of God is committed to communicating it to his pupils. And the teacher who loves children is committed to helping meet their needs. But in the final analysis, the teacher's most important lesson is himself. The teacher who is called of God will want to provide the best example possible for his pupils.

Identification helps to change lives. Young boys learn their role in life by identifying with their father. Later on, they identify with other adult men, hopefully with godly Christian men. The same forces are at work in the lives of young girls. All children should have a godly Sunday School teacher who loves Jesus Christ so that they will be influenced accordingly.

More and more children are coming from broken homes. They do not have a father or mother after which to pattern their life. They should be able to find in their Sunday School teacher a substitute father or mother who has the qualities of Jesus Christ. Children who have never known a Christian father can begin to appreciate the loving care of their Heavenly Father through their Sunday School teacher.

Teachers impart more by actions than by words. Sometimes the way that a teacher squeezes a child's hand says, "I love you," much more than the words they put on a flannelgraph board. Both the words that are spoken and the actions that are symbolized must, of course, reinforce each other.

SUMMARY

A teacher must be careful that he uses the right words, involves the pupils in learning, reaches them through their activities, and makes sure their needs are met, while all the time he is a godly example. This is the teaching process.

Learning is like taking medicine: each person must do it for himself. No one can do it for the pupils. In the same sense, every person must learn for himself the lessons God has intended. The goal of Sunday School teaching is to teach the Word of God to the unsaved, to cause the Christian to grow in Jesus Christ, so that every pupil may be "... a perfect man, unto the measure of the stature of the fulness of Christ" (Ephesians 4:13).

GUIDE QUESTIONS FOR STUDY AND DISCUSSION

1. Give the definition of teaching in Sunday School.
2. Why is lecture/explanation of the Bible an important part of teaching?
3. Name three ways a teacher can involve pupils in the lesson.
4. What is the role of activity in teaching?
5. What is evident in the life of a pupil if the teacher is helping him solve his problems through the Scripture lessons?
6. What is the most important lesson a teacher can teach?

ACTIVITIES FOR FURTHER STUDY AND APPLICATION

1. Have the class members share their testimony of the teacher who has had the greatest influence on their lives. Ask them to analyze why that person had such an impact on them.
2. Have each class member share his idea why Christ was an effective teacher. List the ideas on the chalkboard. Then have the class analyze the suggestions, looking

for a profile of an "ideal" teacher.

3. Make a survey of the evangelistic outreach of your Sunday School. Determine how many students were won to Christ through the Sunday School. A chart showing the number of visits, class growth, special campaigns, will give insight into the soulwinning activities of your church.

RESOURCES

Gangel, Kenneth O., *Understanding Teaching* (Evangelical Teacher Training Association, Wheaton, IL, 1968).

Milton, John M., *The Seven Laws of Teaching* (Baker Book House, Grand Rapids, MI, 1955).

Richards, Lawrence O., *Creative Bible Teaching* (Moody Press, Chicago, 1970).

Towns, Elmer L., *Team Teaching With Success* (Standard Publishing, Cincinnati, OH, 1971).

10 Discipling Through the Sunday School

The New Testament Sunday School begins with lost people and makes good Christians out of them. Jesus described the process: "Go ye therefore, and teach [make disciples of] all nations . . . teaching them to observe all . . . I have commanded you" (Matthew 28:19, 20). This is discipling.

DISCIPLING INCLUDES TEACHING

Since the way pupils are reached determines the way they grow to maturity, discipling concerns itself with the total educational process. A person who is a disciple is technically defined as one who accepts and assists in spreading the doctrines of another. Discipling then becomes *making disciples*—or causing those who have accepted Christ to grow to maturity in their faith so that they can reach others for Christ. Certainly, this is the work of the Sunday School.

DISCIPLING INCLUDES FOLLOW-UP

1. Discipling by follow-up. The Sunday School teacher begins with evangelism. The aim of teaching is that every unsaved pupil be led to Christ. But the teacher's responsibility for that life does not end with his salvation. Jesus did not stop there. He commanded us to teach ". . . them to observe all things whatsoever I have commanded you . . . ." They were to assist in spreading His doctrines. While this includes teaching God's Word in the class, another part is through personal contact outside the classroom.

The total program of follow-up must be as well-planned as the total program of teaching. It cannot be left to chance. We would not bring a baby into the world and give him hamburger one day, milk the next, and allow him to go without food for a week. Nor would we require him to feed himself. Can you see a baby on the kitchen floor with cans, an opener, and a package of frozen food? First he must be fed, then he must be taught to feed himself.

2. Technique of follow-up. One strategy of follow-up is to challenge the new Christian to dedicate his life to Christ. The teacher should watch for selective parts of the curriculum materials that will make the meaning of dedication clear through biblical and contemporary illustration. Some lessons afford the ideal preparation for a direct invitation to make Jesus Lord of the life and to become active in His service and in witnessing. The alert teacher who knows the lives of the pupils will be sure to extend such an invitation. Far too many teachers allow pupils to "come in the front door and go out the back door," never challenging them in the cause of Christ.

Some of the most outstanding preachers in the pulpits today are there because of a godly teacher's direct influence—the teacher who laid a friendly hand on the shoulder of a youth and said, "I believe God can use you in the pastorate." Or, in the case of some others, lives were motivated toward missionary service by a Sunday School teacher who, in effect, made a similar challenge.

But not all who accept Christ will become either

pastors or missionaries. Their discipleship may take one of many other forms. The important factor is their willingness to be and do as God plans for them.

A teacher may become acquainted with the pupil's background and desires. Just as a teacher might walk into a shoe store and win a D. L. Moody to Christ and Christian service, so a teacher may be led to walk into a grocery store and talk with a young clerk about his opportunities to witness in his business. A teacher may visit and carry just the right Christian book for the young Christian to read. He may take the pupil with him to visit unsaved persons of his peer group, affording the new Christian opportunity to observe as the teacher leads the unsaved to Christ.

Some Sunday Schools have a class to teach discipleship. It may be called the "new members" class, but its teaching content is chiefly aimed toward imparting to the new Christians the foundation of and the challenge to be disciples.

Other groups have a combination of class presentation and involvement in service. In a class meeting, the young Christian studies how to go out and be a witness for Christ. He learns what Scriptures to use to bring conviction, how to present the simple plan of salvation, and how to invite the lost person to make a decision for Christ. Then he goes out to the homes of the unchurched with an experienced soulwinner.

More than soulwinning skills are communicated in this apprenticeship experience. Attitudes are communicated, such as love for people, the compulsion of the gospel, and the necessity of tact and understanding. Desire and attitude are other values which are communicated better in service; they are sometimes hard to get across in a formal classroom situation.

3. Absentee Visitation. There is another kind of follow-up which may, in the long run, result in producing discipleship in a person who has confessed Christ but has become lax in attendance. That is visitation of persons who have been absent from classes. Invariably, some of the "faithfuls" will balk at the suggestion that absentee members should be visited. They don't believe in "babying" the chronic dropouts. "We have all we can do to try to reach the prospects," they contend.

But statistics have faces. The total list of absentees for any given Sunday is made up of individuals— individuals like the teen named Debbie who had been absent for a month before the teacher ever contacted her to discover why. By then it was too late. Debbie had backslidden and committed sin which would scar her for a lifetime.

It should never be said of a Sunday School teacher what was blurted out by the mother of eleven, "You're the first Sunday School teacher who ever came to see her." If personal contact is impossible, the telephone is next best. Where there is no phone, a card or letter says, "I really care about you."

DISCIPLING INCLUDES DEVELOPING SPIRITUAL GIFTS

Spiritual gifts are defined in *The Ryrie Study Bible* as "abilities which God gives believers that they may serve Him" (I Corinthians 1:7 note). These spiritual abilities may enhance natural talents with which the believer was born, or they may be supplementary.

To the oft-repeated complaint, "I have no gifts," Paul answers: "Every man hath his proper gift of God" (I Corinthians 7:7), and "But all these worketh that one and the selfsame Spirit, dividing to *every man* severally as he will" (I Corinthians 12:11, emphasis mine). No one can say, there is nothing I can do to serve the Lord; I

125

don't have any gifts. The Bible says that everyone receives gifts and the gifts are chosen by the Spirit, not by the individual recipient. This means that both teacher and the Christian pupil have spiritual gifts.

The successful Sunday School will be concerned with helping pupils discover what gifts God has given them and develop the use of them. A partial listing of these may be found in I Corinthians 12:8-10: wisdom, knowledge, faith, healing, miracles, prophecy, discerning of spirits, tongues, interpretation of tongues. Verse 28 adds helps. In Romans 12:3-8, Paul also lists: ministry, teaching, exhortation, giving, administration and mercy.

The teacher's knowledge of Scripture and of age-group psychology are important in developing gifts. Multi-gifted pupils may tend to seek the limelight to the exclusion of the one-gift pupil. The teacher must seek to lead each pupil to allow God to use and improve his gifts.

At the same time, the Sunday School teacher must make it clear to all that, "As we have many members in one body, and all members have not the same office: so we, being many, are one body in Christ, and every one members one of another" (Romans 12:4, 5). In the body of Christ, as in the physical body of each member, one member may not consider another member inferior. All are part of the same body—and the Sunday School class may well lay a firm foundation for that truth in precept and experience.

Not infrequently the teacher—an objective third party—can discern some gift in the life of the pupil unseen by the pupil's parents. Recognition of a particular gift and the use and development of that gift may spell the difference between developing or losing a pupil. An aggressive junior boy sought recognition through hitting and teasing other pupils. A caring teacher discovered the boy's brilliant mind and fluent reading ability and got him involved in learning activity. Prior to this, the boy had only listened to the lesson. When he received legitimate appreciation, he felt no need for undesirable acts to gain attention.

Within the classroom, the teacher can develop gifts or allow the pupils' growth to plateau. The untrained teacher may feel he must be a "one-man band," performing every duty himself. The trained teacher, agreeing with Paul's advice to Timothy, will commit to students that which he knows, so that the students will, in turn, be prepared to keep the chain of influence unbroken.

A part of the development of the gifts will be the teacher's provision for lesson application and response. Since, for example, *giving* is one of those gifts to be exercised by all believers as a part of worship, the teacher will seek to develop this gift by challenging sacrificial giving in response to a story such as that of the widow who gave all she had. Beginning with small coins brought by young children, the teacher's emphasis of proportionate giving will develop life habits that parents sometimes neglect, possibly because it is not their own practice.

Another gift possessed to a greater or lesser degree by all believers is that of *helps*. Helpfulness can be taught and practiced within the classroom and encouraged beyond its doors. Few traits have been so well stressed through character stories, and a wealth of material is available to reinforce the teaching.

Discovering who has which kind of gift may be a matter of design rather than accident. Some teachers keep a notebook with a page about each pupil. Included on the pages are notes about the pupil's spiritual growth and development. Whether or not it is noted in writing, the alert teacher will make mental notation of pupil response to invitations and opportunities for participation. It may be that the child's spontaneous part in an activity will reveal a special ability.

Child or adult, the teacher's word of encouragement about the use of his gifts may start him on the road to full-time Christian service in the area of his ability. The teacher's emphasis on the importance of using the gifts will focus pupil attention on the need to pray for wisdom to know which gifts have been given to him, and then to make those gifts the best possible, in order to count the most for God.

DISCIPLING INCLUDES RECRUITING FOR SERVICE

"Why aren't our young people dedicating their lives for missionary service?" On occasion, church leaders express this concern. In such situations, they seem unable to see that the young people have no concern for something about which they have comparatively little knowledge. Recruitment for the armed services starts with advertising, unless the draft is involved. The army of the Lord is made up of volunteers and the Spirit often uses information to prod the Christian to volunteer.

Some Sunday School curriculums emphasize missions weekly, others bring a missionary application as the Scripture lesson emphasizes missions. But the church's own missionary responsibilities should be kept before the pupils in numerous ways. When a missionary is visiting the church for a Sunday or longer, he or she should be asked to speak to departments or classes, showing curios from the field and giving a challenge concerning missionary work. Departments or classes could "adopt" a missionary child—or several children from various mission lands—as their special interest for a year. They could write letters, send books or other gifts, decorate their walls with maps and pictures of the country or countries, and in other ways create an atmosphere of missions in Sunday School.

We must re-emphasize that missions and the pastorate are not the only definitions of Christian service. On every hand needs abound for the willing and faithful Christian, calling for all the abilities with which he has been endowed. The teacher must keep alert for opportunities to emphasize ways pupils can serve.

SUMMARY

Discipleship is more than shutting the back door to stop the dropouts of Sunday School. Discipling, as found in the Great Commission, is helping believers in Christ to grow to maturity, and this is one of the great aims of Sunday School for each pupil.

One of the favorite terms for Christians in the Book of Acts is the word *disciples* (Acts 1:15; 6:1, 7; 11:26, 29). Since Christians were called disciples and we are commanded to "make disciples" of those won to Christ, this ministry of discipling becomes paramount. It cannot be left to chance but must be incorporated into the Sunday School's aim, program and basis for evaluation of its success.

GUIDE QUESTIONS FOR STUDY
AND DISCUSSION

1. How would you define discipling?
2. In what way is a teacher's job just begun when a pupil has been led to accept Christ?
3. Name several ways of discipling a new Christian.
4. How does an apprentice disciple learn to serve?
5. In what way is visiting absentees a form of

discipling?
6. What are spiritual gifts and who has been given them?
7. Why is the teacher an important agent in the development of spiritual gifts?
8. How can a church provide more opportunities for their young people and adults to serve Christ?

ACTIVITIES FOR FURTHER STUDY AND APPLICATION

1. Plan a special class for new Christians to acquaint them with the methods and means of discipleship.
2. Plan a project to bring more information regarding missions to your class or department. Be sure to involve many or all pupils in different aspects of the project.
3. Plan a monthly extracurricular activity for youth and adults which will encourage and require the use of their gifts. This could take the form of a service project, such as an activity with and for patients in a nursing home, a party for underprivileged children or beautifying the church in a special way.

RESOURCES

Collins, Gary, *How to Be a People Helper* (Vision House, Santa Ana, CA, 1976).

Ryrie, Charles C., *Balancing the Christian Life* (Moody Press, Chicago, IL, 1969).

Ziegler, Sandra, *Service Project Ideas* (Standard Publishing Company, Cincinnati, OH, 1977).

11 The Laws of Sunday School Growth

Many have attempted to classify principles whereby Sunday Schools or churches grow. Some have arrived at detailed explanations of Sunday School expansion; other formulas are simplistic.

In the past, Sunday School has gone through several cycles—at times experiencing rapid growth, at other times a reversal in attendance. The techniques that produced growth in one generation may not work 100 years later. Some "laws" of growth have been tied to fads. Hence, they should not be called laws because that word implies a timeless principle that spans culture and circumstance. The principles of growth presented here transcend time.

WHY BE CONCERNED ABOUT GROWTH?

1. God expects numerical growth. Sunday Schools should give themselves to numerical growth because God expects a Sunday School to grow. Why?

First, the example of the growing church in Jerusalem allows for growth. "And the word of God increased; and the number of the disciples multiplied in Jerusalem greatly . . ." (Acts 6:7).

Second, the Great Commission, the marching order for the Sunday School, implies growth because when people are won to Jesus Christ and are brought into the Sunday School to be taught the Word of God, there is natural growth.

Third, growth is a reflection of life; things that are not growing are dying.

Fourth, Sunday School growth is the result of the biblical law of fruit-bearing, each producing after its kind. Christians should be producing fruit in their own lives and in the lives of others.

Fifth, Sunday School growth is necessary because a growing world population means that more people need to be reached and won to Jesus Christ. As Sunday Schools grow, more churches are established to meet the need.

Sixth, there should be growth to make a bigger impact on metropolitan areas. To reach our neighborhoods for Christ, we need an organized outreach, more workers, more space, and a larger budget.

Seventh, the growing Sunday School can give a better, well-rounded ministry to the total needs of Christians. The larger the church, the more Christians in attendance; hence, the more people with spiritual gifts to minister to one another.

2. God expects growth in knowledge. Growth is not numerical expansion alone. The farmer is concerned about the produce he ships to the market, but he is also concerned about growth in the tree and perhaps the dollar growth of the business so he may purchase other land.

Sunday School growth is concerned with Bible knowledge. We must reach more unsaved pupils and enroll them so they can be taught the Bible; this is growth in knowledge. "Then they that gladly received his word were baptized: and the same day there were added unto them about three thousand souls. And they continued stedfastly in the apostles' doctrine and fellowship ..." (Acts 2:41, 42). Growth in biblical doctrine results in growth in faith and character by both teacher and pupil.

3. God expects growth in outreach. When persecution scattered the Jerusalem Christians abroad they became missionaries and preached the Lord Jesus wherever they went. In Antioch, "... the hand of the Lord was with them: and a great number believed, and turned unto the Lord" (Acts 11:21). The total Sunday School must grow in its professional ability to minister to pupils.

BALANCING THE LAWS FOR GROWTH

There are four basic causes, or forces, for Sunday School growth. We are calling them the four basic laws for Sunday School growth. They are: (1) the law of outreach; (2) the law of discipling; (3) the law of organization and administration; and (4) the law of leadership.

1. Balancing the four forces. The chart, "Laws of Sunday School Growth," shows four forces of growth: Outreach, Discipling, Organization, and Leadership. Balance is the key to the mature life and Sunday School is no exception to that rule. Each area of growth should be balanced with the other three.

Some Sunday Schools are strong in outreach and may overemphasize busing. As commendable as evangelism is, it is not the total ministry of the church.

Other churches overemphasize discipling with a strong program of teaching and training. But discipling should never overshadow outreach.

The same can be said for organization. Some churches have gone overboard on programming. Every person should fit into a slot and the whole Sunday School should operate smoothly. But when program-

Laws of Sunday School Growth

OUTREACH

NATURAL — Outreach Necessitates More Leadership
Leadership Sets the Pattern & Provides the Vision

FACTORS — Discipling Leads to Outreach
Results Motivate Discipling

Campaigns
Bus Visitation
Advertisement
Letters
Radio & TV

SPIRITUAL

Prayer
Soul Winning
Witnessing
Preaching
Revival

FACTORS

LEADERSHIP

Human
Relationship
Leadership
Skills
Motivation
Supervision

Call of God
Spiritual Power
Dedication

CHURCH GROWTH

Love
Fellowship
Bible Teaching

DISCIPLING

Involvement
Handwork
Applications
Competition

Attendance
habits

CONTRIBUTING — Organization Depends on Leadership
Leadership Values & Promotes Organization

TO GROWTH — Needs Necessitate Organization
Organization Promotes Discipleship

Bible Aims
Bible Standards
Bible Job
Description

Principles of
Administration
Efficient Organization
Proper Buildings
Educational Equipment

CONTRIBUTING

TO GROWTH

ORGANIZATION

Chart adapted from one in *The Successful Sunday School and Teachers Guidebook*, Elmer L. Towns. Used with permission.

ming becomes more important than the other three spokes of the wheel, the Sunday School is unbalanced.

The last spoke is leadership. Lee Roberson, pastor of Highland Park Baptist Church of Chattanooga, Tennessee, says, "Everything rises and falls on leadership." How true that is. But the Sunday School is more than its leaders; it is the body of Christ working together to reach, teach and win its community to Jesus Christ.

When one of these four forces is out of balance, there is no growth. When the body loses its equilibrium, it is sick; likewise, when the Sunday School loses its balance, it stops growing.

2. *Balancing spiritual factors with natural factors.* There are two circles on the chart. The inner circle represents the spiritual factors that contribute to Sunday School growth. The outer circle represents natural factors that contribute to growth. These must work in harmony.

Spiritual factors are forces that the Holy Spirit uses to produce growth. Natural factors are the principles that man uses arising from his native ability that causes a Sunday School to grow. This division of labor causes God and man to work together. Paul reminds us, "For we are labourers together with God" (I Corinthians 3:9). The key phrase is "together with God"—God accomplishing what only He can do and man doing the work given by God—but together accomplishing the work of the Sunday School.

This division of labor is illustrated in farming. First, the farmer must plant the right seed, at the proper time, according to the laws of nature. Then he must wait for rain or arrange for irrigation. He must fertilize and harvest at the right times to secure a good return. On the other hand, only God can cause the miracle of germination to bring forth the plant, then the fruit, and finally the harvest. The better man works with God, the larger the harvest.

The same parallel is true in Sunday School. The staff must arrange proper buildings, equipment must be purchased, and rooms set in order. There must be a well-balanced curriculum that is presented to the pupil at his age level in an interesting manner so that he is motivated to learn. But after a teacher has used all of his training to present the Word of God only the Holy Spirit can work in the pupil's heart to convict of sin and open blind eyes. Only God can produce faith and spirituality. In Sunday School, God and teachers must work together for a spiritual harvest.

Just as the growing human body is an intricate balance of many forces, so the Sunday School must have balance if it is to grow according to God's pattern. People must be growing in Christ; the program must be growing in its ability to meet needs; and the numbers must be growing because of evangelism.

APPLYING THE LAWS FOR GROWTH

Each of the four major laws of Sunday School growth has many expressions or applications.

1. The Law of Outreach: Sunday Schools grow according to the effectiveness of their outreach into the neighborhoods they serve. We cannot wait for the unsaved to come into our church looking for salvation. The Great Commission begins with "Go." Therefore, a Sunday School must reach out of its buildings into the community to make contact with the unsaved with the view of motivating them to give an honest hearing to the gospel.

Spiritual factors in outreach. These factors involve the principles through which the Holy Spirit works in the lives of people: (1) prayer for growth (John 14:14; Matthew 7:7); (2) soulwinning, presenting the gospel in an understandable manner and motivating the person to respond to Christ; (3) witnessing, sharing a personal faith in Christ with others; (4) preaching and teaching, presenting the message with logic and persuasion so that people will respond; (5) revival and evangelistic crusades; and (6) organized visitation, so that the neighborhood is systematically covered and everyone is presented with the gospel.

These are only a few of the spiritual factors that, when faithfully followed, will cause a church to grow.

Natural factors in outreach. These involve advertisement, promotion, and publicity—letting the community know where the Sunday School is located, what its ministry is, and extending an invitation to attend.

Notice on the chart that (1) natural factors include a Sunday School attendance campaign where the pupils are encouraged to bring their friends to Sunday School; (2) the bus ministry involves spiritual factors of soulwinning and natural factors of advertisement, with door-to-door invitation; (3) advertisement includes church or Sunday School newspapers, circular letters, postcards, handwritten letters, advertisements in the local newspaper and on radio, in addition to using community bulletin boards, bumper stickers, billboards, and posters. There are hundreds of natural factors to advertise a church's ministry to the community. The more advertisement used by a Sunday School, the larger the number of visitors—hence, the more who can be won to Christ.

2. *The Law of Discipling: A Sunday School grows according to its effectiveness in teaching and discipling those who attend Sunday School.* The process of discipling is simply making followers, because a disciple is a follower. When a Sunday School does a good job

discipling, students attend its classes because of what they get out of the lessons. This deals with internal motivation or meeting the needs of individuals. Some Sunday Schools have done such an effective job of ministering that this is the foundation of their growth.

Spiritual factors of discipling. Sunday Schools grow because: (1) of the love that people feel one to another; (2) of the enjoyment of fellowship they have in the services; (3) the Word of God is so effectively taught and preached that people are nourished; (4) the filling of the Spirit equips people to serve God, causing churches to grow; and (5) the gratitude people feel to Christ motivates them to attend Sunday School. All of these factors cause Sunday School growth.

Natural factors of discipleship. There are natural laws where people are involved in the teaching-learning process which cause a Sunday School to grow. They are: (1) people attend Sunday School because they are involved in the learning process by good teaching techniques; (2) children attend Sunday School because they are rewarded by activities (handwork) and other educational concomitants; (3) the quality of the practical applications causes people to attend Sunday School because their lives have been changed; (4) students attend Sunday School because of competition and other means of motivation to bring out their best; and (5) pupils should develop the habit of attending Sunday School so that it becomes natural for them to come every Sunday morning.

3. The Law of Organization: A Sunday School grows according to its ability to organize and administer its program to meet the needs of all its members. Some workers resist any attempts to organize the Sunday School because they think programs kill the spirit of Christianity. However, there were programs in the New Testament. Programming is simply putting the right person at the right place with the right tools to do the right job at the right time. The apostles "daily in the temple, and in every house . . . ceased not to teach and preach Jesus Christ" (Acts 5:42). There is evidence of time (daily), place (in the temple and every house), plan (they ceased not), and program (to teach and preach).

Spiritual factors of program. The Sunday School (1) must be organized around a biblical aim, (2) must have placed itself under the authority of the Bible, (3) must be guided by spiritual leaders (laymen must have their proper place of responsibility), and (4) there must be biblical standards so that the chain of command is followed. "Let all things be done decently and in order" (I Corinthians 14:40).

Natural factors of program. Many churches are poorly organized, are run in a haphazard manner. Under this point, the principles based on truth that would help any organization be efficient can be applied to the church. A well-organized church enlists, trains, and properly directs its workers. The principles of properly using educational buildings and equipment must be followed. Then there will be harmony of effort and spirituality of results.

4. *The Law of Leadership: The Sunday School grows according to the effectiveness of its leaders to perform their jobs in carrying out the aims of the Sunday School.* The leader is the length and shadow of the work he builds for God. We cannot build our Sunday Schools on Madison Avenue public relations men and methods; we must begin with the man of God. Leadership begins with the pastor, flows down to the superintendent, department superintendents and, finally, to every Sunday School teacher. Leadership is getting the job done through other people. If the job isn't getting done, there is no leadership.

Spiritual factors of leadership. These are: (1) the

leader must be called of God; (2) he must meet the biblical requirements in his personal life; (3) the leader must be empowered by the Holy Spirit to accomplish his job; (4) he must have an understanding of biblical principles and be able to apply them to the ministry of the Sunday School; and (5) he must be a man dedicated to prayer.

The spiritual factors all contribute to growth, but Sunday Schools do not grow unless they are tempered with leaders who are able to get things done on a day-by-day basis. Some leaders are "so heavenly-minded they are of no earthly good." Therefore, there must also be natural factors in good leadership.

Natural factors of leadership. The person in a place of leadership (1) should understand basic human relationships and how to get along with people; (2) he should understand how to motivate people to get the job done; (3) he must know how to train people, both technically and in informal settings; (4) have the ability to supervise and evaluate workers; and (5) understand how to solve interpersonal problems, produce a cohesive staff, and keep everyone working toward the goal.

Now, studying the chart again, notice once again how the four laws affect and balance each other. Outreach results in motivating discipling, while discipling leads to outreach. Discipling needs necessitate organization, while, conversely, organization promotes discipleship. Organization depends on leadership, and good leadership values and promotes organization. Leadership sets the pattern and provides the vision for outreach and outreach necessitates more leadership.

Keep these four forces in good balance and the Sunday School is bound to grow.

SUMMARY

The laws of Sunday School growth are never automatic; they must be applied. The work of Sunday School goes forward with human effort that is anointed of God. These four laws must be equally balanced for New Testament growth, including proportionate attention to outreach, discipling, organization, and leadership. Then there must be equal stress on spiritual and natural factors.

Some Sunday School growth may be from superficial causes, such as advertisement only. Such increase in numbers cannot be denied but is not New Testament in nature.

GUIDE QUESTIONS FOR STUDY AND DISCUSSION

1. Where should the Sunday School get its principles of outreach?
2. Why should Sunday Schools want to grow?
3. Why is balance important?
4. What is the difference between spiritual and natural factors in growth?
5. List and explain the four major laws of Sunday School growth, giving attention to both the spiritual and natural factors involved in each.

ACTIVITIES FOR FURTHER STUDY AND APPLICATION

1. Have the class analyze their Sunday School to determine the strongest and weakest expression of the four laws of Sunday School growth. How can the

weakness be overcome?
2. Have the class analyze the best Sunday School outreach programs/campaigns during the past few years. What made them effective? Could they be conducted again?

RESOURCES

Getz, Gene A., *The Measure of a Church* (Regal Books, Glendale, CA, 1973).

Lawson, E. Leroy and Tetsunao Yamamori, *Church Growth: Everybody's Business* (Standard Publishing, Cincinnati, OH, 1973).

Towns, Elmer L., *America's Fastest Growing Churches* (Impact Books, Nashville, TN, 1972).

Wagner, Peter C., *Your Church Can Grow* (Regal Books, Glendale, CA, 1976).

12 Sunday School's Bright Future

During the decade of the sixties, Sunday School attendance declined in many churches. Leaders felt the pressure of failure and began experimenting with innovative techniques to attract pupils back to Sunday School. There were tangents of group dynamics, programmed education, and educational television. Also, there were experimental classes in social issues, play activity classes, sex education, and sensitivity training. Alternate programming, such as "Wednesday Schools," or diversified cell classes were tried.

None of these experiments were evidently successful; efforts that appealed to the pupils' fancy or efforts tied to fads apparently did not work. But the Sunday School refused to die. It grew in churches where traditional methods were used, where the Bible was taught as God's Word and lives were changed. Sunday morning was found to still be the best meeting time, when the largest group of people have time available to pursue an organized study of the Bible. Also, it is the time when people expect churches to offer religious education.

Sunday Schools that are the most successful are those that have gone back to the basics. The newest innovation in Sunday School is a return to past workable forms. The ways that have worked in the past still apply, but this does not mean we are slavishly tied to every past technique. The eternal principles that are found in the

Word of God are still effective, but they must be re-applied in every generation. It is of value, therefore, to take a quick look at the history of Sunday School to obtain a long-range perspective of its worth and future.

A GLIMPSE IN THE REARVIEW MIRROR

It has frequently been said that "Necessity is the mother of invention," and this was the case with Sunday School. There was a need, and the first Sunday School class was an 18th century Englander's attempt to meet that need.

Robert Raikes, acclaimed the founder of Sunday School, was editor of *The Gloucester Journal* in Gloucester, England. He took both his influential position, which he had inherited from his father, and his religion seriously. He was concerned about people, especially the poor who were often arrested for trivial offenses; he wrote frequent editorials about the conditions they faced in the city's crowded jails. But he did more. He put feet to his convictions and visited the jails himself, passing out Bibles and reading the Word to those who could not do it for themselves.

Raikes' personal life, however, was far different from that of the men and women he visited in the jails. He was well-groomed, a meticulous dresser; so careful was he of his appearance that some called him "Buck Raikes, the dandy."

Raikes' attention to detail carried over to the clean, comfortable home he had provided for his family. It was with plans to further enhance the beauty of this home that, one afternoon, he set out for the slum district in search of a gardener. While there, he was severely jostled by a gang of ragged boys. He mentioned the confrontation to a lady in the neighborhood.

"You ought to see them on Sunday when the factory is closed and they have nothing to do but get in trouble," she responded.

His imagination was stirred. Evidently the slum boys were becoming a growing threat to the district. Conviction gripped Robert Raikes' soul. Here were the children of those he had been working with in the jails. Left to their own devices these children had become half-wild creatures whose lives were filled with hate, fear, and ignorance. What was to be done for them?

He went to Reverend Thomas Stock and together they collected the names and addresses of about 90 children in the area. They visited the families and frequently were cursed for their efforts. But they persisted. Gradually they succeeded in gathering a small class which met in the kitchen of Mrs. Meredith, the first Sunday School teacher.

And so the first Sunday School began; but it was different from our Sunday Schools of today. For one thing, the teachers were paid; indeed, this was almost a necessity considering the challenge they faced. The curriculum was different, too. The slum children were illiterate and had to be taught how to read and write. As they learned, they were encouraged to use these new skills in studying the Word of God. The length of the classes was much longer also. A two-hour session began each Sunday morning at 10:00 and was followed by a short break. Then, after another teaching period, the students were escorted to church.

Discipline was a special problem in that first Sunday School. The group was rowdy and experienced in the ways of mischief. On occasion a student would become so unmanageable that Raikes would escort him to his home, wait as the offender's parent administered the appropriate punishment, then bring him back to class to finish the day's lessons. But the ways of a lifetime were not easily unlearned, and soon the group became too much for Mrs. Meredith. She resigned her post and the class moved on to the kitchen of Mrs. Critchley.

Lives consistently exposed to the truths of God's Word do not remain unchanged, however. As the seeds of Scripture planted in these young hearts began to take root, changes became evident in their lives. In time, Robert Raikes' Sunday School areas became the most orderly in the city of Gloucester.

When Raikes saw the indisputable evidence of transformed lives he began promoting Sunday School in his newspaper. In just four years, Sunday School enrollment in England reached 250,000 children, and by his death in 1811, approximately 1,250,000 children in Great Britain were being reached weekly by Sunday School.

Raikes' influence for Sunday School did not stop with Great Britain. News of this successful new ministry spread to other continents. John Wesley urged, "There must be a Sunday School wherever there is a Methodist society."

Today there are many who believe that it was John Wesley, rather that Raikes, who was the true founder of Sunday School. They maintain that in Savannah, Georgia some 50 years earlier Wesley began instructing children in the Word of God on Sunday afternoons. This is true. Wesley's classes, however, could not technically be termed Sunday School because his efforts concerned the children of Christians—catechism instruction and the aim of edification.

A true Sunday School has four unique characteristics: (1) it reaches the unsaved as well as Christian children; (2) instruction is given from the Word of God rather than the oral question and answer drills of catechism; (3) its purpose is to evangelize the lost as well as to instruct the saved; and (4) it is operated by laymen rather than by clergymen. The unique nature of Sunday School itself discounts Wesley's claims and reinforces Raikes' position as founder.

The first recorded American Sunday School was started in 1785 in Oak Grove, Virginia, by William Elliott. Another Sunday School appeared in Virginia in 1786. Rapidly, Sunday Schools began to spring up in South Carolina, Maryland, Rhode Island, New York, and Pennsylvania. Just 11 years after Robert Raikes started the first Sunday School in England, a new Sunday School Society was organized in Philadelphia, Pennsylvania. Within three months this group raised $3,968 for the establishment of new Sunday Schools.

Around 1829, the Mississippi Valley enterprise captured the imagination of Sunday School leaders in the East. The region west of the Alleghenies to the Rocky Mountains was practically void of religious influence despite its four million population. The American Sunday School Union spearheaded a massive evangelistic thrust to reach this area with the gospel. In May, 1830, they resolved to start a Sunday School in every town in the Mississippi Valley; they wanted to complete this project in two years. Two thousand people supported and promoted the project, including such well-known figures as Daniel Webster and Francis Scott Key.

Over 80 missionaries were sent out to establish Sunday Schools in the Midwest; one of these was a man who himself had been reached for Christ through the American Sunday School Union. "Stuttering Stephen" Paxson had overcome the double handicap of a limp and a stammer to become a successful hatter and the favorite fiddler for the Saturday night square dance in the little town of Winchester, Illinois.

"I'll get a star if I bring a new scholar to Sunday School," said his little daughter Mary. "Will you be my scholar, papa?" she begged. Paxson was a good husband

and father and he was soon coaxed into becoming little Mary's "scholar."

Paxson's first visit to Sunday School was different from most. Rather than being a mere spectator he was immediately saddled with the responsibility of teaching a boys' class. Somehow, with much coaching from the boys, he made it through the morning's lesson. The class period had been a tremendous struggle for Paxson and he was relieved when it was over. The boys, however, had enjoyed having Paxson as their teacher and begged him to return the following Sunday. He finally agreed, but only on one condition: he would teach the same lesson again, only this time he would do it right.

This was only the beginning for Paxson, for as he studied to prepare those Sunday School lessons week after week, he met the God of the Bible. As Paxson learned more about God's Word, he caught the vision of the American Sunday School Union and moved his family to the Mississippi Valley. There he and his horse, appropriately named Robert Raikes, set out to establish Sunday Schools. Over the next 25 years the two traveled 100,000 miles, stopping to speak to any child they passed. In the 1,314 Sunday Schools established by this zealous missionary, 83,000 children were reached for God.

During the next 50 years, 80 percent of all the churches in the Mississippi Valley came out of Sunday Schools. Between 1824 and 1874, 61,299 Sunday Schools were organized, reaching 2,650,784 young people for Christ.

The Sunday School movement was growing, but there were problems. There was no printed Sunday School material so each teacher taught the Word of God as best he could. In many cases the pastor would instruct the teachers at the weekly meeting, and on Sunday the teachers would present the identical lesson to their pupils. This alleviated the problem to some extent.

Immediately following the Civil War, Sunday Schools radically changed. In 1866, John H. Vincent, a Methodist minister of Chicago, published *The Sunday School Teacher* containing "a new system of Sunday School study," with analytical and illustrative helps for teachers and lesson helps for pupils. B. F. Jacobs, also of Chicago, urged in a Sunday School convention in 1872 the idea of uniformity of lessons (prior catechism lessons had been graded to some extent). Vincent's new lesson plan and Jacobs' plan of uniformity were adopted. They were used by various denominations and were published in secular papers and religious weeklies. *The Sunday School Times,* a weekly newspaper, became a main vehicle to spread the Sunday School lessons throughout America. At one time, it had the largest circulation of all magazines in the United States. Churches in Canada became interested and the system of lessons was soon adopted also in Great Britain, and within a few years they were being used in as many as nineteen nations as The International Uniform Lesson. Many millions of people were studying these lessons by 1900, and the lessons are credited with the period of great progress in the Sunday School throughout the world.

In spite of their popularity and widespread use, not everyone was satisfied with the uniform lessons. It was claimed that they did not provide comprehensive, consecutive and complete knowledge of the Bible and they did not allow for denominational doctrinal differences. Others urged that the graded principle be recognized, with lessons more suitable to young children. Eventually an all-Bible graded series of lessons was worked out by Clarence H. Benson by the early thirties.

The Sunday School conventions, which had been

organized earlier, began to grow after the Civil War years. These conventions were, in actuality, massive rallies where laymen motivated each other to do the work of Sunday School. Small committees worked on resolutions, strategy, and plans; but little attention was paid to practical techniques. The conventions were, in fact, large-scale revival meetings and made great impact on the cities in which they met.

In the early 1900s, however, Sunday Schools in great numbers turned from spiritual horizons to academic ones. Liberalism crept into theological seminaries and sifted down to the churches and ultimately affected the Sunday School. The Sunday School convention eventually became the International Council of Religious Education under the liberal World Council of Churches.

A little girl once asked, "If Sunday Schools used to be so big, why doesn't everyone go now?"

That is a good question. Why has Sunday School lost the influence it once had? Let's make the answer simple enough for a little girl to understand.

When Sunday Schools taught the Word of God, people attended because they wanted to know what God was saying; but when they neglected the miracles and denied that Jesus was the Son of God, Sunday Schools became like every other school—so children would just as soon stay at home and play. Attendance went down; Sunday Schools had lost their influence.

A LOOK TO THE FUTURE

The Sunday Schools that are growing today are those that believe and teach the Bible as God's holy Word. The Great Commission is still our marching orders for Sunday School—people reaching people for Jesus Christ.

A football coach has told his players, "The future is NOW." By that, he motivated them to action. Some of the latest trends in Sunday School are a return to old workable forms. Some may be good; all need to be weighed in the balance for their greatest effectiveness in individual schools.

1. Innovations that are based on a return to previous methods. There is renewed emphasis on a "high attendance day," whereby the entire Sunday School staff gives optimum effort to generating interest in Sunday School. This is an innovation of the historic rally day which had the purpose of rallying Sunday School enthusiasm. The high attendance day accomplishes: (1) new attenders; (2) absentees return; and (3) enthusiasm.

There is a return to opening exercises in some schools, but they are given a new title, such as *assembly, worship,* or *pre-lesson* periods. Some teachers feel the pupils need learning readiness before they can begin instruction.

The large auditorium Bible class is making a comeback because many adults are intimidated by visiting a small class and becoming involved with strangers. In the large class, they enjoy anonymity, yet they are exposed to a systematic presentation of Bible exposition.

Bible memory activities are returning in the form of flannelgraphs, overhead transparencies and memory games. The golden text is no longer stressed but the need for memory work is felt.

The pupil's manual is being used more extensively as a classroom teaching aid. Pupils are answering questions and expressing themselves on paper. At the same time, the traditional manual is not being used so much as homework; teachers sometimes keep the manuals in the class until the series is completed.

The use of puppets is bigger than ever. A few years ago Sunday School was about the only educational school using puppets. But with the emergence of Sesame Street and educational television for children, puppets have proven to be an effective method of instruction.

The use of Sunday School banners, posters, and room decorations is sweeping Sunday Schools. It is said, "The walls have ears," but they also can speak, and a decorated room in keeping with the theme reinforces the lesson.

The International Uniform Lessons continue to lose their appeal, yet many churches want all pupils to study the same lesson so Sunday School learning can be tied to family devotions. Yet there are drawbacks to "uniform" and "unified" grading curriculums as shown in the chapter on curriculum. With such a weakness as lack of Bible coverage during a pupil's life, churches might do well to encourage family devotions around a book of the Bible, or by some other method which gives additional Bible exposure, rather than combining it with the Sunday School lesson.

Pocket books are popular as Sunday School texts, especially for young people and adults. Yet this can hardly be called a new trend. The American Sunday School Union printed over eight million small pocket-size texts in the 1800s. Pocket books seem to become more popular each year, however.

For the past 100 years, Sunday School curriculum has been dated for correlation. Now there seems to be more demand for a non-dated curriculum that can be reused. This means the teacher can become proficient in teaching specific lessons and Sunday School can correlate its lessons by content. The Sunday School curriculum was nondated for its first 75 years.

2. Innovations that are reapplications of Bible principles. The master teacher method of teaching could be a new form of the classes conducted by Robert Raikes, but the learning psychology and teacher motivation are different. One teacher with several associates is teaching groups of 25 to 60 children in larger rooms. This method, as we have discussed, is called *modified team teaching* or *open session teaching.*

The Board of Christian Education will make a greater impact because churches feel a need to pre-plan, coordinate, and evaluate their total educational program with a view of improving its ministry.

The "split-level" Sunday School is also called *double session,* whereby the same facilities are used two or three times on Sunday morning with a different staff for each session. This has become an answer for the need of facilities for fast-growing Sunday Schools.

A graded children's church program during the morning service is growing in its acceptance, especially in churches with an extensive busing ministry. Children's church can be correlated to Sunday School or can be separate as the adult church service is separate in Bible subjects.

Special classes are being organized and attempts are being made to provide literature for instruction of the deaf, retarded, blind, and those from foreign or cultistic backgrounds. Also receiving attention are the divorced, the single adult, professional groups, senior citizens, and other special groups.

In the Sunday School of the future more men will be teaching younger children rather than leaving this responsibility to women only. The classrooms will become larger, better illuminated, with age-graded, plastic-molded furniture. There will be more rugs on the floors with emphasis on comfortable surroundings. The small cubicle classroom of 10' x 10' is not being built as often as in the past because the size of classes is getting larger and more room is needed for learning activities.

Emphasis in the future will be on open space and a cheerful atmosphere.

The Sunday School room of the future will have larger chalkboards, tack boards, maps, overhead projectors, and other visual aids. There will be interest centers in the children's division—such as for worship, various activities, nature, role play, and books, puzzles, and games. The classroom will have built-in flexibility and expandability for more than Sunday morning use.

The classes of the future will make greater use of films, especially film cartridges. The use of videotapes, closed circuit television, and programmed education are probably still off in the distant future. Visual aids will be used by average laymen, so the implementation of sophisticated equipment will be limited by personnel and cost.

Tape cassettes will have a larger role in Sunday School teaching, especially to bring in messages from outside authorities, music, sound effects, and testimonies.

Small grouping will continue to grow in effectiveness and use, including buzz groups, dyads, listening teams, study groups, circular response, symposium, and colloquy.

Sunday School busing enjoyed mushroom growth in the early seventies even though it had been around since the thirties. It began as "convenience busing"; churches began providing alternate transportation for those without it. The biggest growth came when bus workers went door-to-door to reach the lost and win them to Christ; this was the beginning of "evangelistic busing."

Many churches got into the bus ministry but began to abandon it when its cost became prohibitive due to the Arab oil embargo in the mid-seventies; when they realized it was hard work and they were not willing to sacrifice; and when other concomitant problems, such as overcrowding, discipline problems, and de-emphasis on numbers, made it difficult. But Sunday School busing is still effective and will probably continue to expand among those Sunday Schools willing to pay the price of hard work.

The Sunday School conventions are having a good contribution. Whereas they were interdenominational in the past, today most Sunday School workshops and institutes are sponsored by denominations. However, there still are large interdenominational conventions that encourage the work of Sunday School. Also, specialization has influenced the movements. Today there are Sunday School gatherings that emphasize one of the following: teaching methods, growth, visual aids, Vacation Bible School, church libraries, bus ministry, etc.

SUMMARY

God has promised to bless His Word. Sunday School, therefore, has a bright future when its programs and methods are based on the Word of God. However, there have been times of growth and decline in the history of Sunday School. When innovative ideas are not biblical, or are not practiced in keeping with the times, Sunday Schools will decline. The Sunday School's future is tied to the Bible it teaches and the authority of Christ who empowers it.

GUIDE QUESTIONS FOR STUDY AND DISCUSSION

1. What did Sunday School leaders do in the sixties to halt the decline of Sunday School attendance?
2. Why did these efforts fail?
3. What were the motives of Robert Raikes in beginning Sunday School?
4. What were the aspects of Raikes' Sunday School that qualify him as the founder of Sunday School?
5. What significant changes in Sunday School occurred about the time of the American Civil War?
6. Why are some latest innovations in Sunday School that are effective similar to previous workable methods?
7. List the new methods that will work best in your Sunday School.
8. Why do you think Sunday School has a bright future?

ACTIVITIES FOR FURTHER STUDY AND APPLICATION

1. Even though the term *Sunday School* is not found in the Bible, the principles are there. Think through the Scripture and list the activities that are similar to Sunday School. Make a list of biblical words that communicate things done in Sunday School.
2. Examine your Sunday School workbooks to determine the up-to-date activities suggested.
3. Review the objectives of Sunday School in chapter one; then determine how true Sunday School has been to its aims throughout its history.

RESOURCES

Benson, Clarence, *A Popular History of Christian Education* (Moody Press, Chicago, IL, 1943).

Eavey, C. B., *History of Christian Education* (Moody Press, Chicago, IL, 1964).

Towns, Elmer L., *A History of Religious Educators* (Baker Book House, Grand Rapids, MI, 1975).